THE BUTTERFINGERS ANGEL

MARY & JOSEPH HEROD THE NUT & THE SLAUGHTER OF 12 HIT CAROLS IN A PEAR TREE

an entertainment by
WILLIAM GIBSON
author of "The Miracle Worker"

designed and illustrated by
ELLEN KEUSCH

PAULIST PRESS
New York / Ramsey / Toronto

Library of Congress Catalog Card Number: 76-22280
ISBN: (paper) 0-8091-1890-4; (cloth) 0-8091-0198-X

Published by Paulist Press
Editorial Office: 1865 Broadway, N.Y., N.Y. 10023
Business Office: 545 Island Rd., Ramsey, N.J. 07446

Printed and bound in the United States of America

Acknowledging . . . Diane Romano who cared about type . . . Harry Shore, Karon Plummer and Jean Thomas of the printers, Thomson-Shore, Inc., and John Kirvan who conceived the book and Tom Intondi who produced it.

To all the infants in the world
—W.G.

For John, another kind of angel
—E.K.

House lights on.

The Cast enters down the aisle to the beat of a drum, greeting the audience. There are three Kings, bathrobed and crowned, each with a gift-package—gold, white, and black; the 1st King leads by halter a sedate little Cow, and the 2nd a frisky Sheep who keeps jumping on his back, and the 3rd a young lady in a green sheathe-dress and fur coat. They are followed by two barefoot peasant Women with washbaskets underarm, out of which they bestow confetti on the audience. There is a handsome Man In Grey who does nothing. He is followed by Joseph and Mary, arm in arm; Joseph is in carpenter's apron and Mary in bridal-veil, washbasket underarm, out of which trailing sheets are carried as a train by a young Girl; they are followed by an Angel, a boy in white with a promptbook, which he is nervously studying. The rear is brought up by a small Donkey, beating a large drum. It's an impromptu parade, and anything else may happen on it that amuses the actors.

Onstage, in a chorus-line front, they begin a syncopated clapping; the stage lights steal up on them.

CAST: (*single voices, chorus on refrain*)
Fill the stage with bits of folly,
Fa la la la la, lala, la la.
Sing with us, the time is jolly,
Fa la la la la, lala, la la.
So we wear our gay apparel,
Fa la la, lalala, la la la,
Acting out an old-time carol,
Fa la la la la, lala, la la.

Play a much-told tale before you,
Fa la la la la, lala, la la.
We trust in God the plot won't bore you,
Fa la la la la, lala, la la.
Let us add, if we offend,
Fa la la, lalala, la la la,
The moral is our ways to mend,
Fa la la la la, lala, la la.
(*Fading away.*)
Fa la la la la, lala, la la.
Fa la la la la, lala, la la.
(*They drift back to sit at rear.*)

House lights off, stage lights on.

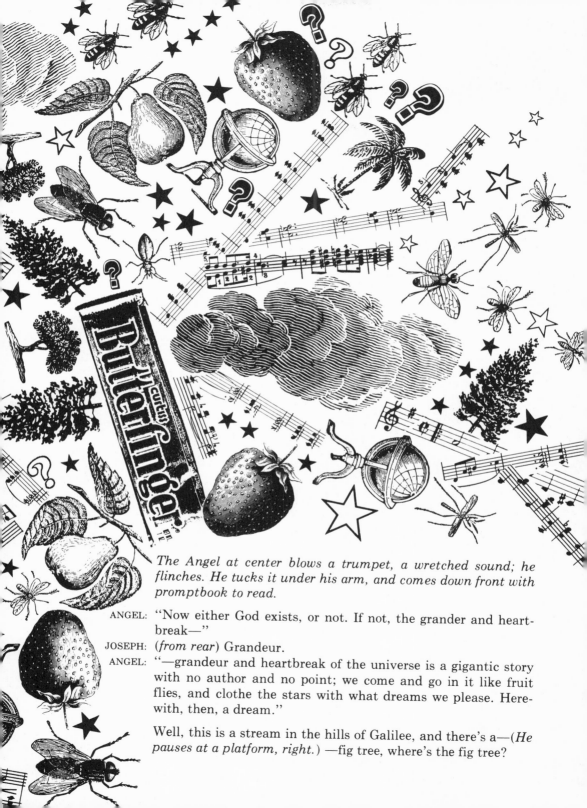

The Angel at center blows a trumpet, a wretched sound; he flinches. He tucks it under his arm, and comes down front with promptbook to read.

ANGEL: "Now either God exists, or not. If not, the grander and heart-break—"

JOSEPH: (*from rear*) Grandeur.

ANGEL: "—grandeur and heartbreak of the universe is a gigantic story with no author and no point; we come and go in it like fruit flies, and clothe the stars with what dreams we please. Here-with, then, a dream."

Well, this is a stream in the hills of Galilee, and there's a—(*He pauses at a platform, right.*) —fig tree, where's the fig tree?

This is a strean

n the hills of Galilee, and—where's the fig tree?

YOUNG LADY: (*from rear*) Coming. (*She comes down wrapped in her fur coat, a rather narcissistic Tree. The Angel helps her up a step.*)

ANGEL: No coat, please—

TREE: My branches.

ANGEL: Branches— (*He runs to get two leafy branches; she models the coat for us.*) Now. It's springtime, and—

TREE: (*snuggling her cheek*) It's December.

ANGEL: It's springtime in this dream and all the trees are in leaf, here. (*She takes the branches; the Angel pulls at her coat, she pulls back.*) No coat, we—

TREE: It's my bark!

ANGEL: We said no coats, if—

TREE: That was weeks ago—

ANGEL: —if you'll please—

TREE: —a sunny afternoon in October—

ANGEL: —do as we agreed in October—

TREE: I just got this coat for Christmas!

ANGEL: (*pauses*) Is that what this story is about?

TREE: It's about Christmas, certainly, it's about Christmas and joy—

ANGEL: It's not about fur coats!

TREE: What's it about?

ANGEL: It's about God. Now will you please do as I say?

TREE: Are you God?

ANGEL: I am the Angel of the Lord—

TREE: Only God can make a tree, I don't have to do what you say.

ANGEL: (*controls himself*) Then will you kindly be in leaf?

TREE: Yes. (*She graciously spreads her branches,*
and the coat slips from her shoulders;
the Angel snares it.)
ANGEL: Thank you.
TREE: That's not fair!
ANGEL: You do have to do what I say,
the whole climax of the story depends on it.
TREE: (*muttering*) See about that.
ANGEL: What?
TREE: (*sweet*) I said, we'll see.

(*The Angel shifts the coat, trumpet, and promptbook, and reads.*)

ANGEL: "But if God is—

"—*if* God is, we are in a story whose author, his point unknown, is the fire in every star, fruit fly, and man; in the sentence of things created—"

JOSEPH: (*from rear*) Sentience.

ANGEL: "—sentience of things created—we see only the back of his hand. Which in pity for our blindness, some believe, turned and fingered the birth of himself as a man among us, so in one face we might see the fire and live. Herewith, then, the birth."

Well.

(*The Angel blows the trumpet, no better, and dropping the promptbook; the Cast sings, and Joseph rises to his name, as three women—the third a businesslike adolescent, Mary without veil—pick up their washbaskets, and carry them down left.*)

CAST: When Joseph was an old man,
An old man was he,
He married virgin Mary,
The queen of Galilee;
He married virgin Mary,
The queen of Galilee—
(*They continue to hum.*)

JOSEPH: (*humbly*) Good morning, Mary. (*Mary turns to him; the two Women kneel down left to scrub and talk.*) I was—passing by—

MARY: Joseph, you've got to stop following me around. (*The humming breaks off.*)

JOSEPH: I try.

MARY: No, you try to pass by.

JOSEPH: Yes.

MARY: And then you don't pass by, you get stuck.

JOSEPH: Yes. I am stuck in an old man's hunger. I know, a girl of delicacy, people talk, and you—

MARY: I don't care if people talk, you're just wasting your time.

JOSEPH: (*winces*) Not if I see your face like a violet once a—

MARY: Face, your eyes crawl all over me like ants.

JOSEPH: —once a day in this empty desert.

MARY: What desert, it's Galilee.

JOSEPH: Of my life.

MARY: Oh, poetry? Joseph, I know what you want—

JOSEPH: I'm as prosaic as anyone! a hard worker with a steady income and a fine house I hate to go home to alone, every piece of furniture in it made by me for a family God has never sent: but poetry, my child, is not even the prophets, it is the tongue of the living spirit, and its word here is not my simile but you.

MARY: —and the answer is no.

JOSEPH: You think I am too old for you, an old man who—

MARY: Old men, young men, they're all the same to me. I don't want to get married. And if I did, I wouldn't want to marry you.

JOSEPH: Why?

MARY: You're too old for me. (*She joins the other women, kneeling to scrub.*)

JOSEPH: She isn't even logical. Illiterate, callous to poetry *and* money, a heart like a stone in an icy brook, and her ankles are too fat, great God in heaven, why have you confused my old eyes with this hunger for young flesh? (*The Angel is searching worriedly in the folds of the fur coat for the promptbook; Joseph picks it up.*) Here.

ANGEL: *(much relieved)* Oh, thank you.
       It's the Annunciation—
JOSEPH: Send a boy to do a man's job—
       (He goes to sit at rear;
       the Angel looks for his place.)

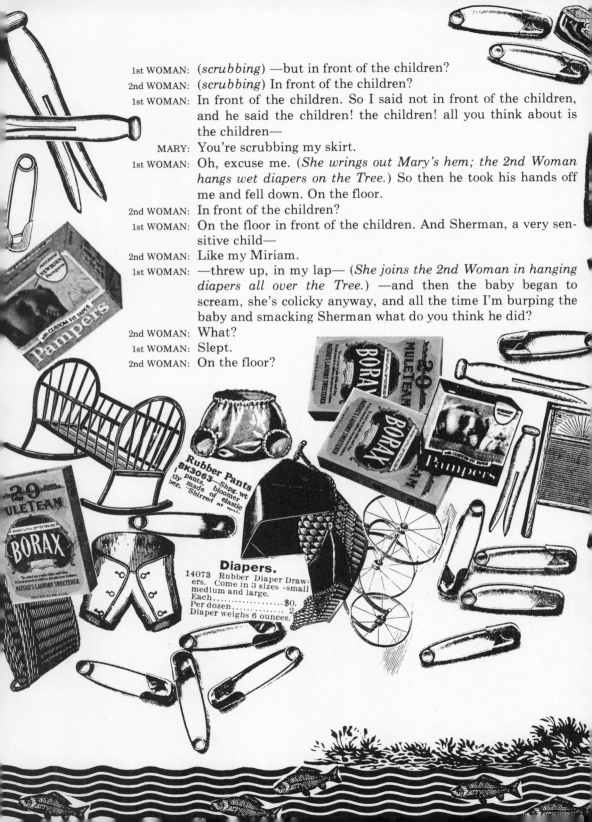

1st WOMAN: (*scrubbing*) —but in front of the children?

2nd WOMAN: (*scrubbing*) In front of the children?

1st WOMAN: In front of the children. So I said not in front of the children, and he said the children! the children! all you think about is the children—

MARY: You're scrubbing my skirt.

1st WOMAN: Oh, excuse me. (*She wrings out Mary's hem; the 2nd Woman hangs wet diapers on the Tree.*) So then he took his hands off me and fell down. On the floor.

2nd WOMAN: In front of the children?

1st WOMAN: On the floor in front of the children. And Sherman, a very sensitive child—

2nd WOMAN: Like my Miriam.

1st WOMAN: —threw up, in my lap— (*She joins the 2nd Woman in hanging diapers all over the Tree.*) —and then the baby began to scream, she's colicky anyway, and all the time I'm burping the baby and smacking Sherman what do you think he did?

2nd WOMAN: What?

1st WOMAN: Slept.

2nd WOMAN: On the floor?

1st WOMAN: Like a log. I was up walking the baby all night stepping over his face, he said it was the best night's sleep he ever had. (*She hangs a last diaper on the Tree's face; the Angel takes a deep breath behind Mary to read.*)

MARY: If I ever get married I hope my head explodes. (*The Angel is left open-mouthed.*) Or have babies either.

ANGEL: Er—

1st WOMAN: Listen to her.

MARY: How can people live the way people live?

2nd WOMAN: What way?

MARY: What way, listen to her!

1st WOMAN: Little Miss Know-it-all. You'll get married.

2nd WOMAN: And have babies too, why do you think you're born with all those things inside?

1st WOMAN: And outside.

ANGEL: (*embarrassed*) Ladies—

MARY: I wasn't born just to make more babies to make more babies, that's circular reasoning! I think everybody is different, I'm different, and the difference is who I *am* inside, not all those things, and I think we're born to make the most of the difference, I will too—

2nd WOMAN: You're different, all right, you're cracked.

ANGEL: Ladies—

1st WOMAN: Is that a coat?

ANGEL: Is what a coat?

1st WOMAN: That animal thing.

ANGEL: Oh, this. Yes. It's a coat for—
(*The two women come to examine it; Mary scrubs.*)
—ladies who are cold in their hearts—

2nd WOMAN: I never felt anything so soft in my life—

1st WOMAN: Beautiful, what kind of animal is it?

ANGEL: I think it's some kind of rabbit.

TREE: (*muffled*) Rabbit!

2nd WOMAN: Are you selling them?

1st WOMAN: Can I try it on?

ANGEL: Take it with you. (*He gets rid of them upstage with it; the Tree shakes her branches violently, and the Angel hurries to pick off the wet diapers.*)

TREE: (*testy*) Catch my death of cold here, I'm the one needs the coat—

ANGEL: Go, go get it back—

TREE: He's right, send a boy to—

ANGEL: —and please stuff it in your mouth? I have enough problems here. (*The Tree goes upstage, recaptures the coat, and sits. The Angel throws the diapers into the empty washbasket nearest him, with the trumpet; Mary is spreading her wash on*

a platform, left; the Angel signals, the lights change, and the Cast gives him a celestial hum. Then the Angel reads.) "Hail, thou that art highly favoured, the Lord is with thee: blessed art thou among women." (Mary turns.) "For thou hast found favour with God. And behold, thou shalt conceive in thy womb, and bring forth a son, and shalt call his name Jesus. And he shall be great, and shall be called the Son of the Highest; and he shall reign over the house of Jacob for ever: and of his kingdom there shall be no end."

MARY: What? (The Angel signals, the Cast gives him another celestial hum.)

ANGEL: "Thou has found favour with God. And behold, thou shalt conceive in thy womb, and bring forth a son, and shalt call his name Jesus. He shall be great—"

MARY: What?

ANGEL: Mary, I can't go on repeating this time after—

MARY: Who are you?

ANGEL: I am the Angel of the Lord.

MARY: (pause) You're a boy.

ANGEL: Yes.

MARY: You're only a boy—

ANGEL: No.

MARY: (*pause*) You said, conceive, what?

ANGEL: "Conceive in thy womb, and bring forth a son, and—"

MARY: (*indignant*) Have a baby?

ANGEL: Yes.

MARY: Like them?

ANGEL: No.

MARY: I can't, I haven't got a husband like them, thank God.

ANGEL: Not like them, and not—

MARY: I haven't even got a boy friend!

ANGEL: —like any child ever. Listen.

MARY: I hate boys, you must have the wrong Mary.

ANGEL: "The Holy Ghost shall—" I beg your pardon?

MARY: I said you must have the wrong Mary.

ANGEL: (*worried*) Is that possible?

MARY: Possible, there's three Marys just on my street, everybody is named Mary! that's the trouble with this town, people get the same ideas over and over—

ANGEL: Oh, I—I am sorry—

MARY: What for?

ANGEL: My mistake, I—

MARY: Everybody makes mistakes here.

ANGEL: No, I make too many, it's not only here. They know how I get things wrong, they said this time get it right or don't come back.

MARY: Don't—?

ANGEL: Come back.

MARY: Your nose is sweating!

ANGEL: Yes, when I make a mistake.

MARY: I won't tell anybody, stop sweating.

ANGEL: Thank you. (*Mary picks up the washbasket, the Angel hunts in the promptbook.*) I was looking for—

MARY: Act more confident, for an angel.

ANGEL: I—had it here—

MARY: Look confident you get more things right, it's how I do, most people don't know the difference anyway—

ANGEL: 21 Hadeganim Street?

MARY: Two blocks north and up the hill, the third shack on the left, the door's off one hinge.

ANGEL: Yes, you're very confident.

MARY: I ought to be, it's my house. (*She turns to leave, and lets the washbasket drop.*) Oh, my—

ANGEL: Mary. (*She turns back to him; they stare at each other.*)

It's a virgin birth

MARY: (*finally*) You see?—you were right!

ANGEL: Yes.

MARY: (*points up*) *They* were wrong!

ANGEL: No.

MARY: Yes, if I haven't got a husband or boy friend or—

ANGEL: No.

MARY: —*something* male—

ANGEL: It's a virgin birth.

MARY: A what?

ANGEL: Listen, Mary. "The Holy Ghost shall come upon thee, and the power of the Highest shall overshadow thee: therefore also that holy thing that shall be born of thee—"

MARY: Without even asking me?!

ANGEL: "—shall be called the Son of God. For with God nothing shall be impossible."

MARY: I have other plans!

ANGEL: What plans?

MARY: To go to Jerusalem, I'm saving every cent—

ANGEL: You'll go to Jerusalem.

MARY: —to make something of myself!

ANGEL: Mary, be still! I tell you God is to be born of your womb, and live on the earth as a man, and all men shall see in him the love that shakes the stars, and you have other plans?

MARY: I do, I do, give up everything I thought of all my life, for what? (*She snatches up her wash, throws it in the washbasket.*)

ANGEL: A firstborn Son.

MARY: Diapers!

ANGEL: Who will light the world.

MARY: That's what they all think! Let it be Sherman, I'm not going to *be* like them, dumb as cows and stuck here drooling the rest of my life, I'm not! Why me?

ANGEL: I have no idea.

MARY: Go back and tell them I said never. (*She stalks out of the light with her wash, up left.*)

Without
even
sking me?

ANGEL: I can't go back! They said— (*But he is alone. He closes the
promptbook, drops it, and gazes up into the lights here and
there.*) God? God?

I don't see what to do.

God, it is very dark on the earth, and if I can't see my way,
how can these creatures? they—have not much light in them,
and they do each other harm in the dark. Oh, I know you know
that, it's why your light is to become flesh, so that men will
live more joyously in love than in hate, and see one another as
themselves, but this—girl who complains of how people live is
a brat. God, you can't make a silk purse out of a—(*He thinks
better of it.*)

Well, I think there's been a mistake, *not* mine. And if so, and
I'm not to come back till it's right, it will be dark here for some
time. Is that what you want?

God?

God, if you're always silent, how shall I know you hear?
Answer me!

(*The Sheep wanders down right—*)
SHEEP: Baaa.
(*—and begins to drink at the stream.*)

ANGEL: Don't drink there, it's polluted.
SHEEP: Oh?
ANGEL: They were just washing diapers in it.
SHEEP: What's wrong with them?
ANGEL: They don't see others as themselves, upstream is safer.
SHEEP: Thank you.
ANGEL: Don't mention it. (*The Sheep goes left to drink, and Mary walks back with the washbasket.*)

MARY: I thought it over. (*The Angel turns.*) I'm sorry I lost my head, that's how sometimes I think things over. (*The Angel waits on her, she is scowling.*) Let's sit down.

ANGEL: Of course. (*Mary inverts the empty washbasket down front, sits on it; the Angel does likewise with his full one, sits. The Sheep curls up at Mary's feet, listening.*)

MARY: I heard what you said.

ANGEL: Oh, I am sorry—

MARY: Don't keep apologizing, I am a brat.

ANGEL: I was speaking to someone else—

MARY: He never answers you?

ANGEL: No.

MARY: I don't think he's out there.

ANGEL: (*jumps up*) You're an atheist too?

MARY: Did you ever see him out there?

ANGEL: No.

MARY: I thought you were so important.

ANGEL: Oh, no. It's—infinite, this is a small dark room in a palace that's infinite, the important ones are—out with him in—

MARY: I don't think he's out, I think he's in. I know why it's me.

ANGEL: You do.

MARY: It's to start with me because— See, I'm not the only brat, there's eighteen in my family, all with black beards except me. It was nineteen but the baby fell in the fire and died, only she didn't fall, they were drunk and threw her in.

SHEEP: Tsk, tsk, tsk.

MARY: It's like living with crazy wolves, you better be a brat. I'm surrounded by morons, I hate everybody I know. And I shouldn't. (*The Angel sits again, slowly.*) See one another as themselves, did you make that up?

ANGEL: No.

MARY: So it's to start with me. (*The Angel stares.*) How do we begin?

ANGEL: It's begun.

MARY: Besides, I always get things right, I mean nobody wants a baby with three feet, especially this one. So I— (*She stiffens, knuckles her heart.*) Ooh. Ooh. (*The Cast takes up her ooh, oooooh, like a rising wind; the Sheep cowers.*) I'm scared, I never— never was so scared in all my life, why am I so *scared?*

ANGEL: Mary. (*He falls at her feet, kisses them.*)

MARY: Hold my hand! (*The Angel grips her hand.*) Oh God, let him be healthy and happy, I don't care if he's all that special or even a girl, just let me deserve this baby! (*The wind dies away. Mary lets the Angel's hand fall, blinks.*) Did I say that?

ANGEL: Mary, I'm scared too, hold *my* hand.

SHEEP: Hold *my* hand.

ANGEL: It's a—terrifying thing we—

MARY: Terrifying, what'll I tell my family? (*She jumps up, the Angel in tow.*) They'll kill me in that house—

ANGEL: You can't go back there, they—

MARY: I live there, where'll I sleep?

ANGEL: —they throw babies in the fire. (*Mary's eyes widen on him.*) I'll speak to Joseph.

MARY: (*blankly*) Joseph.

SHEEP: (*incredulous*) Joseph?

MARY: (*resigned*) Joseph—

ANGEL: Mary, from now on I'll take care of you.

MARY: And I'll take care of you, I have to go now— (*She makes for the washbasket, the Angel after her.*)

ANGEL: No, be careful!

MARY: (*startled*) What?

ANGEL: Don't lift any—heavy objects—

MARY: I'm healthy as a whale—

ANGEL: (*firmly*) No. (*He gets the washbasket from her; the lights begin to include the others.*) I'm responsible for this baby.

MARY: (*reluctant*) Well. Just don't spill it, please.

ANGEL: Mary, you must be more—trusting now—

MARY: I know.

ANGEL: And humble.

MARY: I am humble, it's my strongest point— (*They go upstage left, Mary ahead, the wash spilling out of the basket alongside the Angel.*)

(*The Sheep and the Cast sing,
the Sheep taking the tags solo.*)

SHEEP, CAST: Joy to the world! the Lord is come, *come, come,*
Let earth receive her king, *little thing,*
Let every heart, *take heart and start,*
Prepare him room, *let diapers bloom,*
And heaven and nature sing, *dingaling,*
And heaven and nature sing, *dingaling,*
(*They get stuck.*)
And heaven, and heaven—
And heaven, and heaven—
And heaven, and heaven—
And heaven, and heaven—

(The Sheep skips off, left. From the right a Girl and two other Children run down to pick up the two inverted baskets, and the diapers underneath the Angel's; they spy the trumpet, and halt.)

GIRL: Look.

1st CHILD: Where'd that come from?

2nd CHILD: Your mother takes in trumpets? *(The Girl picks up the trumpet, and tries to blow it; a handsome Man In Grey comes down from back as the others reach for the trumpet.)*

2nd CHILD: Lemme try—

1st CHILD: No, me, me, I'm next—

GIRL: Finders keepers, finders— *(They see the Man approaching, and freeze; when he puts his hand out for the trumpet they back away down left, in a terrified huddle. The Man smiles at them. The Angel returns from up left, picking up the spilled wash.)*

MAN IN GREY: You failed to mention me.

(The Angel looks from the Children to the Man, puzzled.)

ANGEL: Who are you?

MAN IN GREY: They seem to know. Am I too soon? (*He crosses to the Children, very gentle, and bends to proffer a handful of coins. The Angel heads for his promptbook, right. The Children each take a coin slowly; the Man takes the trumpet.*) Now give me a kiss, and take your things home. (*They peck at his cheek, hurry to the baskets, and run with them off right; the Angel is leafing in the promptbook.*)

ANGEL: Are you in this?

MAN IN GREY: Oh, I think so. (*He comes back, trumpet in hand.*) It's an interesting idea, this birth, if you can bring it off.

ANGEL: If?

MAN IN GREY: Well, I foresee difficulties, as always. Joseph's reluctance—

ANGEL: He's not reluctant.

MAN IN GREY: He will be. And of course the usual hazards of wilderness travel, and childbed fever in an unsanitary milieu, and crib deaths—

ANGEL: These things aren't happening—

MAN IN GREY: Oh, many infants die in the crib, some by accident. And some slaughtered, so I don't myself regard this birth as a foregone conclusion, do you?

ANGEL: Well, I'll—do everything I—

MAN IN GREY: "And of his kingdom there shall be no—"?

ANGEL: End.

MAN IN GREY: No end, I doubt that too. Here, you lost your trumpet.

ANGEL: Oh, thank you.

MAN IN GREY: I thought it was my cue, they blow it almost as well as you. Though of course, it's always my cue. (*He bows slightly, turns to go up left.*)

ANGEL: (*worried*) Am I going to have any trouble with you?

MAN IN GREY: Yes, but I don't think I'll have any with you.

(*Joseph comes down left with a plank, saw, and tape-measure; the lights lose the others at rear as he saws, at the platform.*)

MAN IN GREY: Ah, Joseph, work, work, work, where is the fun in your life?

JOSEPH: (*the saw keeps sticking*) Fun?

MAN IN GREY: Women.

JOSEPH: Where indeed.

MAN IN GREY: Perhaps you're wise, getting on and hardly a lover, and they're a lascivious lot.

(*He goes up left out of the light; the Angel has retreated right, the trumpet and wash under his arm, hunting his place in the promptbook.*)

JOSEPH: (*pondering*) Are they? (*He is about to saw, stops.*) If they're so lascivious why has it not come to my attention?—virtue everywhere! And in that little violet's eye did I ever see a glint of it? —never. (*He saws again, stops.*) Oh, Joseph, that assumes you are the man to tempt her eye. If they're not so lascivious how do these swarms of infants get underfoot?—copulation everywhere. Well, what does her eye see? (*He wipes the saw, uses it as a mirror, and stares.*) A grey-faced old goat, that's what, and worse, a comical old goat, you dream of nibbling at that violet? —marry you, she'll be fluttering her eyes at every *young* goat in town. What a life, I've had a narrow escape. (*He puts the saw on the plank, and brushes off the floor with his hand to lie down.*) Work, work, work, yes, and go to bed with the prophets. (*The Angel approaches, takes a deep breath behind him to read; Joseph yawns.*) I *am* wise, if I ever marry her I must remember, commit suicide at the wedding.

(*The Angel is left open-mouthed. Joseph dozes off snoring; the Angel flings the promptbook down and clutches his hair, but controls himself.*)

ANGEL: Be calm. Follow instructions. Wipe your nose. (*He blows and wipes his nose in the wash, and retrieves the promptbook; he returns to stand above Joseph and reads.*) "Joseph, thou son of David, fear not to take unto thee Mary thy wife: for that which is conceived in her is of the Holy Ghost. And she shall bring forth a sin—"

JOSEPH: (*in his sleep*) Son.

ANGEL: "—son, and thou shalt call his name Jesus: for he shall save his people from their sins."

JOSEPH: Sons.

ANGEL: Sins!

JOSEPH: (*rolls over*) What a nonsensical dream.

(*Up right the little Cow is pursued back and forth by three bearded Louts with clubs, pursued in turn by Mary with a candle; they speak a guttural language, ancient furioso, not very intelligible.*)

1st LOUT: Hud droof tuh konner, schmock!

2nd LOUT: Three shtumpf tuh, goot a shtumpf?

3rd LOUT: Nah goot a shtumpf, schmock, shy three uh clobe?

1st LOUT: Doh why stuh figh clobe!

2nd LOUT: Ull hud droff tuh konner!

3rd LOUT: Hud droof, hud droof!

MARY: Leave that cow alone! (*The Cow lies down at right in surrender, feet in the air; Mary gets between her and the Louts.*) Back, back!

1st LOUT: Um shtoffed!

MARY: It's not your cow!

2nd LOUT: Shtuhbee brake foost!

3rd LOUT: Gahd why, Maggie!

1st LOUT: Um shtoffed!

MARY: Just because you're hungry you can't eat the first cow you meet!

3rd LOUT: Gahd why, Maggie, ull smoosh uh skole!

1st LOUT: Smoosh uh skole!

2nd LOUT: Gahd why ah brake foost!

MARY: Help! (*The Angel hurries to open an as-if door near the Cow, who scrambles in; Mary shakes her finger in the 1st Lout's face.*) Go home or I won't cook you another crumb!

1st LOUT: Wah!

2nd LOUT: Wah!

3rd LOUT: Wah! (*Mary slips in, the Angel closes the door; they listen, apprehensive, with the Cow.*)

1st LOUT: Goon toofuh, Maggie!

2nd LOUT: Nux tom smoosh uh skole!

3rd LOUT: Nux tom, nux tom, wozzit nux tom alla tom— (*The Louts go off up right, growling; the lights there fade out.*)

—and the furniture's just lovely, Joseph.

Now this room with all the junk—

MARY: My brothers, will I ever be glad to get out of this town.
ANGEL: Certainly not the right influence, how come you have brothers like that?
MARY: Doesn't every girl? Did you tell him?
ANGEL: Oh, yes. There *is* a problem, he—doesn't— (*But Mary is off exploring with the candle, opening as-if doors to peek in; the Cow explores after her.*)
MARY: What a mess. (*She takes the tape-measure from the plank, sets down the candle, and stands on the platform right to measure the air; Joseph rubs his eyes, sitting up.*)
ANGEL: (*hissing*) —doesn't want young men around— (*He slips around behind the platform center, the Cow with him, and they peek out; Joseph regards Mary in astonishment.*)
JOSEPH: What are you doing here, child?
MARY: Measuring.
JOSEPH: What for?
MARY: Curtains, it's a really nice house and the furniture's just lovely, but we have to make some changes.
JOSEPH: We, what—
MARY: Is this where you sleep?
JOSEPH: It's where I sleep when people don't march in and—
MARY: I'll clean it up, we can't have all this sawdust now, the— (*She jumps down.*) —baby'll be eating it.
ANGEL: (*hissing*) Don't jump!
MARY: I'll sleep in there, a good coat of whitewash—
JOSEPH: (*rises*) You'll sleep—
MARY: In there, a—
JOSEPH: Where?
MARY: The nursery. Now this room—
JOSEPH: You propose to sleep here?
MARY: No, there. Joseph, don't get young ideas, I'm going to marry you but that's all.
JOSEPH: You're going to—
MARY: Now this room with all the junk—
JOSEPH: (*roars*) You're going to *what?*
MARY: (*stops*) Marry you, I thought he told you.
JOSEPH: Who?
MARY: The angel.
JOSEPH: The *who?*
MARY: Joseph, are you hard of hearing too? I might as well know the worst—
JOSEPH: I am not hard of hearing! I do expect in common conversation a rational thread I can follow—
MARY: Well, I'm going to marry you, it's very rational—

JOSEPH: You are not going to marry me.

MARY: Oh yes I am, I changed my mind.

JOSEPH: Why?

MARY: Because they threw the other baby in the fire.

JOSEPH: Mary.

MARY: So I know I need a good and decent man instead.

JOSEPH: I see. Instead of—some baby they threw in—

MARY: Some, it was my sister!

JOSEPH: Instead of your sister.

MARY: No, instead of my brother, I think maybe you're him, and that's why.

JOSEPH: That's why *what?*

MARY: I changed my mind. Joseph, you're not very logical.

JOSEPH: Mary, I think you're—upset, now sit down and I'll make a cup of warm tea, to calm—

MARY: See, I'm right.

JOSEPH: Yes, absolutely, just—

MARY: You are good.

JOSEPH: —sit down, and I'll—

MARY: I'm not upset. I made up my mind, Joseph, I'm going to marry you and that's final. Now this room—

JOSEPH: (*thunders*) Sit down! (*Mary is taken aback, sits on the platform right.*) If you are not upset, I am! Have you another excuse for invading this—castle, don't raise your eyebrows, a man's home is his castle, waking him up in the night with these incoherent mouthings and plans to turn his house upside down and marry him, will he nill he, like a witch on a broomstick? I would be insane to let you into this house! You are either very upset or an insufferable whelp, now take your choice and make it upset, because I itch to put you across my knee and beat some manners into your bottom with a board!

MARY: Joseph, you have a terrible temper, that's nice.

JOSEPH: Nice!

MARY: It gives me more confidence in you. And a wonderful vocabulary, the things you'll teach him! I thought you were wishy-washy, I guess you wanted to make a good impression?

JOSEPH: (*no longer*) I *did*.

MARY: You made a bad impression.

JOSEPH: *I* made a bad impression.

MARY: Yes.

JOSEPH: *I* am not very logical—

MARY: I'm glad you think so too, let's take one thing at a time, why would you be insane?

JOSEPH: (*it chokes him*) Because I—think of nothing but you all day long, you here, you there, where is she now, what is she wear-

ing, who is she talking with—whom!—

MARY: Marry me you'll know.

JOSEPH: (*grimly*) Will I? Will I? Mary, I am too old for you and *that's* final.

MARY: Who told you that?

JOSEPH: You did.

MARY: When?

JOSEPH: This morning.

MARY: That was this morning.

JOSEPH: Yes, this morning.

MARY: Well, people don't stay the same age, you know.

JOSEPH: What?

MARY: I'm older already. It isn't birthdays, you get older if things happen to you and a thing like this that never happened to *anyone* makes you even older.

JOSEPH: What are you saying now?

MARY: What, he didn't even tell you that?

JOSEPH: What?

MARY: I'm going to have a baby. (*Joseph stands rigid, and closes his eyes, and then heads for the platform center; the Angel and the Cow duck down. Joseph returns with a bottle and a shot-glass. He takes them to the platform left, sits, pours and downs a shot, pours and downs another, pours a third.*) Is that tea?

JOSEPH: No. (*He is about to down the third, changes his mind, brings it to Mary.*) Here, no doubt you need it too.

MARY: Thank you, Joseph. (*She lifts it to her lips.*)

ANGEL: (*on tiptoe*) No alcohol! (*She hands it back.*)

MARY: I'm not allowed. (*Joseph downs it.*)

JOSEPH: Now. When are you expecting the child?

MARY: I think around Christmas.

JOSEPH: Who is the father?

MARY: There isn't any.

JOSEPH: I didn't say husband, I know there is no husband—

MARY: Everybody knows I don't have a husband.

JOSEPH: Yes. I asked who is—

MARY: That's what I thought you'd be.

JOSEPH: Thank you. I do understand it now, you are in trouble and I want to help—

MARY: I'm not in trouble.

JOSEPH: Who is the father?

MARY: There isn't any.

JOSEPH: (*shouting*) Who is the father?

MARY: Gabriel!

JOSEPH: Gabriel. Gabriel who, who is Gabri— (*The Angel comes from behind the platform, with trumpet and promptbook.*)

ANGEL: I'm here, Mary.

JOSEPH: (*staggered*) What is he doing in my cupboard!

MARY: Trusting, be trusting, that's what you said, I'll speak to Joseph, you didn't tell him anything.

ANGEL: I did, I—

JOSEPH: You get in here, you—little villain— (*He marches the Angel by an arm twist down left, the trumpet dropping; Joseph bends him over the platform. The Cow behind the other is astonished.*

COW: Homo sapiens?

MARY: Joseph, be careful, he's an angel.

JOSEPH: He's a villain!

ANGEL: I appeared—

MARY: You don't know who he is—

JOSEPH: I know who he is, I've seen him loitering after you—

ANGEL: I appeared to him—

JOSEPH: —and now I know why!

ANGEL: (*shaking the promptbook*) —in a dream, it says appear to him in a dream.

JOSEPH: You predatory good-for-nothing pipsqueak of a father, *you* seduced this child?

MARY: Did he?

JOSEPH: Don't you know? How many possibilities are—

ANGEL: I did, I did—

JOSEPH: Aha!

MARY: Did he appear to you in a dream?

JOSEPH: No, he did not appear to— (*He stops; then he flops the Angel over to stare at him.*) He did appear to me in a—

MARY: So he told you.

JOSEPH: Yes—

MARY: Let him up. (*Joseph releases him, the Angel slides to the floor; Mary kneels to fan his face with the promptbook.*)

JOSEPH: He said fear not to take unto thee Mary thy wife, for—they're a lascivious— No, that was the other. Did I have two dreams?

MARY: Joseph, apologize.

JOSEPH: You are not the father. (*The Angel shakes his head.*) I apologize. Who is the father? (*The Angel points up; Joseph looks up; the Angel takes the promptbook from Mary, hands it to him open to read.*) "For that which is conceived in her is—" (*He stares at it.*)

ANGEL: (*weakly*) Is of the Holy Ghost.

JOSEPH: The phrase in the dream.

MARY: (*rises*) You remember now?

JOSEPH: Oh, yes.

MARY: Now this room with all the junk—

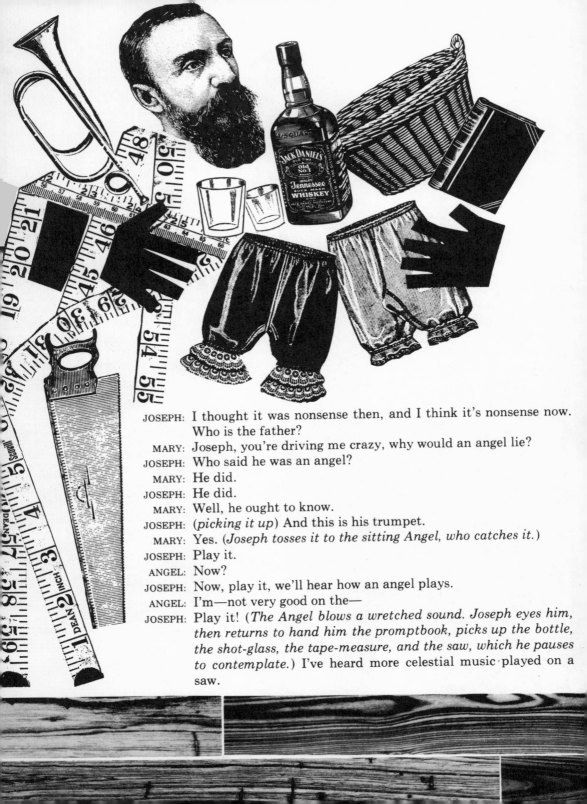

JOSEPH: I thought it was nonsense then, and I think it's nonsense now. Who is the father?

MARY: Joseph, you're driving me crazy, why would an angel lie?

JOSEPH: Who said he was an angel?

MARY: He did.

JOSEPH: He did.

MARY: Well, he ought to know.

JOSEPH: (*picking it up*) And this is his trumpet.

MARY: Yes. (*Joseph tosses it to the sitting Angel, who catches it.*)

JOSEPH: Play it.

ANGEL: Now?

JOSEPH: Now, play it, we'll hear how an angel plays.

ANGEL: I'm—not very good on the—

JOSEPH: Play it! (*The Angel blows a wretched sound. Joseph eyes him, then returns to hand him the promptbook, picks up the bottle, the shot-glass, the tape-measure, and the saw, which he pauses to contemplate.*) I've heard more celestial music played on a saw.

(He carries the things to the platform center and stands staring the Cow in the face across it; Joseph covers his eyes, and when he removes his hand the Cow is gone.)

NGEL: *(low)* I'll—speak to somebody else—

MARY: I want Joseph.

SEPH: Is there a cow here?

COW: *(unseen)* No.
(Joseph comes back with the wash, staring at a pair of red pantalets.)

SEPH: Is this mine?

MARY: How did that get here? Joseph, you love me!

SEPH: That is the only fact in this fog of—senility, perhaps, or alcohol? or I may still be dreaming, or this town has flown off the earth. Here, I must lie down now. You did say you are having a baby.

MARY: Yes.

SEPH: If you are here now come back tomorrow. *(He opens the door, waits for them to leave; the Cow trots around the platform—)*

COW: *(to the Angel)* Shalom. *(—and out past Joseph.)*

SEPH: I think I am lying down now.

שלום
(Shalom)

MARY: Joseph, close the door and I'll tell you the truth. It—won't be easy. (*She indicates the platform right; Joseph sits.*) There's a —married man, I can't tell you his name because it would break somebody's heart, he's very well off, a millionaire, and handsome in a wild kind of—

JOSEPH: Where did you meet him?

MARY: Out of town, I was on a long trip with one of my crazy brothers and he stopped there this night, to see him on business, a big rich house—

JOSEPH: What business?

MARY: I didn't hear, it was a *very* big house, and they sat in the corner sipping imported wine and he never looked at me once, until finally my brother staggered up and said c'moon Maggie—he thinks my name is Maggie—and then *he* said oh Mary is staying with me tonight and he looked at me with such eyes that, well, my lungs just collapsed and he said isn't she and I said yes and my brother went home. Well, it was very disappointing, I'd heard so much about it and with him so handsome I was surprised it was so disappointing, but I had to find out and I found out and now since I got home the—way it is with women isn't—

JOSEPH: How did you get home?

MARY: I walked.

JOSEPH: Far?

MARY: Joseph, don't snoop, there are reasons I—

JOSEPH: Whose heart would it break?

MARY: His widow.

JOSEPH: He's dead?

MARY: Yes, he died very suddenly.

JOSEPH: You said he's well off.

MARY: Yes.

JOSEPH: Dead?

MARY: I didn't think he'd die so suddenly—

JOSEPH: And who is this boy?

MARY: His nephew. Now, the important thing—

JOSEPH: I like the first story better.

MARY: (*a silence*) Joseph, I see I'll have to tell you the true truth. I— have this red-headed girl friend who—

JOSEPH: (*rises*) —is the nephew of an angel who became a millionaire by roasting all the bastard babies in the world for chestnuts, have you the faintest inkling of what the word truth means?

MARY: Joseph, I don't care if I tell lies! If you can't hear the truth with your own ears, fine, I can do without it, because there's something more important, and that is I'm going to have a baby, can you hear that, I'm going to have a baby and I need help and *it* needs help, and I'm going to get what it needs with or without the truth!

JOSEPH: I believe you.

MARY: Now I'm not worried what people say, I'm trying to like them better but they're such dumbbells who cares, I do care what he hears them say. I don't want him to hear that word.

JOSEPH: Which word?

MARY: Bastard, and that's one reason I'm going to marry you, the others are you're a strong and good man, I like you a lot better since we talked, and yes, a good provider, so he'll be healthy, and another is you're smarter than me, he'll learn everything you know about what poetry is and the prophets and love too, because the most important is—you love me. Now. What do you get. I'm young and I work like a horse, I cook for you and wash your clothes and keep this house spotless, I don't turn a thing upside down till you say go ahead turn it upside down, and I sleep wherever you say, and with you if you still want me, but not till this baby is born, and you come home to me and him instead of this empty house and we will both love you, it'll be full of the noises of—all of us growing, and I have never been with another man and I will never be with another man until I die, if you will have us. And that's final. You think it over. (*She picks up whatever wash she has dropped.*) I am here tonight, and thank you, I'll come back tomorrow. (*She goes out. Joseph stands motionless.*)

(The Angel gets up with trumpet and promptbook, but is stopped when Joseph turns and falls to his knees.)

JOSEPH: Oh God, help me. I see her as mine only, and I'm not what she thinks, I'm not strong, only you know what a weakling you made me, envious of men and frightened of women and not good, only you know how evil, and even the love she counts on is more of my self than of her. God, help me to be what she thinks I am.

(The Angel scans the air above Joseph, waiting.)

ANGEL: No answer. *(He turns the promptbook in his hand.)* And not a word of it in the script, I might as well throw it away. It's dark down here, but—interesting—*(He eyes Joseph.)*

It's tomorrow, Joseph. *(Joseph gets up heavily, crosses to the candle, and pinches it out; he takes up the plank in both hands like a woman, rocks it.)* Or next week, or the month after, or however you measure time here.

JOSEPH: Who is the father?

ANGEL: God.

JOSEPH: *(nods)* Of all his children, I mean who is the father of *this* child.

ANGEL: Time is flying, we—

JOSEPH: *(looks up)* Is this the family you send me?

ANGEL: —can't wait for that answer—

JOSEPH: The answer is yes. *(He begins slowly to dance with the plank.)*

(The Angel mounts the platform right, his hands aloft with trumpet and promptbook, triumphant.)

ANGEL: Let the wedding rings bell, wedding bells ring, out! (*An organ booms out with the Mendelssohn wedding march, and Mary, white-veiled and pregnant in an apron, enters to meet Joseph at the center platform for a marriage ceremony; the Cast spills downstage, clapping their hands in a dance around them.*)

(The Angel draws Mary down left, shouting inaudibly.)

CAST: She named him King—*(All freeze in silence, staring at a Courier down right with upraised hand.)*

MARY: *(shouting)* What?

ANGEL: *(shouting)* I said goodbye, my work is done!

MARY: You're—talking too loud, I can't hear you—

ANGEL: I'm going back.

(The Courier with his staff comes among the Cast—he is the Man In Grey but does not know it, bow-legged and gruff, with a coarse poncho over his grey costume—and drops a letter-carrier's pack off his shoulder.)

COURIER: I'm sorry as hell to break up this party but I've only got a minute, and there's a lot of other towns up here to get the word to.

1st WOMAN: What's the bad news this time?

COURIER: There's a new— *(He digs a beribboned paper out of the pack.)* —decree from Caesar. That all the world should be taxed.

2nd WOMAN: What, again?

CAST: *(an uproar)*
More taxes!
Smoosh uh skole!
I'm still borrowing to pay last year's tax!
Joost uh whack uh foe gumpt!
He's driving the business out of this country!
Smoosh uh Caesar skole!
He'll hear from my son the accountant about this!

TREE: I was told this coat's a tax-free gift!

2nd WOMAN: What's he think we're made of, money? Look at this child's feet, they don't even match. Curtsey, Miriam.

(*The Louts threaten the Courier with their clubs.*)

1st LOUT: Gahd tone!

2nd LOUT: Smoosh uh skole!

3rd LOUT: Gahd tone oh smoosh uh skole!

COURIER: Fellers, I don't make the bad news, I just bring it. Now you boys have a hungry look, you related to the bride?

1st LOUT: Yah!

2nd LOUT: Lull sist!

COURIER: So if things get tough you can eat the baby. You can't fight city hall, somebody's got to pay to improve the roads—

1st WOMAN: If he didn't improve the roads *you* couldn't get in here!

JOSEPH: We think the roads are satisfactory as they are.

COURIER: Well, you'll get a look at them. Where's your family from?

JOSEPH: Bethlehem.

COURIER: Back to Bethlehem, and take up the roads with Herod the nut, you'll be right near him. And he just loves babies. (*He scowls at the paper.*) All this gobbledygook— It's a census, folks, ev-

erybody gets to see the old home town again, sign up there by the first of the year. Or off with your heads! Now, I've got some jewelry here, all hand-made by African slaves, I don't do this for a living, just a sideline, that's how I can let you have it so cheap—

(*The Cast clusters around him and the pack; Joseph comes down left to Mary and the Angel.*)

MARY: Joseph, I can't go to Bethlehem,
I just whitewashed the nursery!
JOSEPH: I will go, little melon. I hear you are leaving us?
ANGEL: Yes.
MARY: No—
JOSEPH: Soon, I hope?
ANGEL: Now. (*He goes up to join the cluster, which is drifting up right; the lights lose them.*)
MARY: You've hurt his feelings again. Joseph, I don't think you should go either.
JOSEPH: What do you think I should do?
MARY: I think you should write Caesar a letter, telling him I just whitewashed the nursery. And you can't leave me all alone now.
JOSEPH: You are not all alone, there's your seventeen brothers—
MARY: Brothers, they're never going to *see* this child!
JOSEPH: And when shall I? (*He pats Mary's belly, sings, puts his ear down.*)
O tell me, little baby, when thy birthday will be?
O tell me, little baby—
MARY: Ah, Joseph, you like him. (*She holds his head against her.*)
I want you to be with us.
JOSEPH: Then come.

(*The Angel returns, the Louts at his heels.*)
ANGEL: He says the roads are terrible.

MARY: I said I can't—
1st LOUT: Snot mat uh rose!
2nd LOUT: Maggie ah proptee!
3rd LOUT: Doh go oh smoosh uk skole!
JOSEPH: What are they struggling to say?
MARY: It's not a matter of the roads,
I'm their property, if I go they'll—

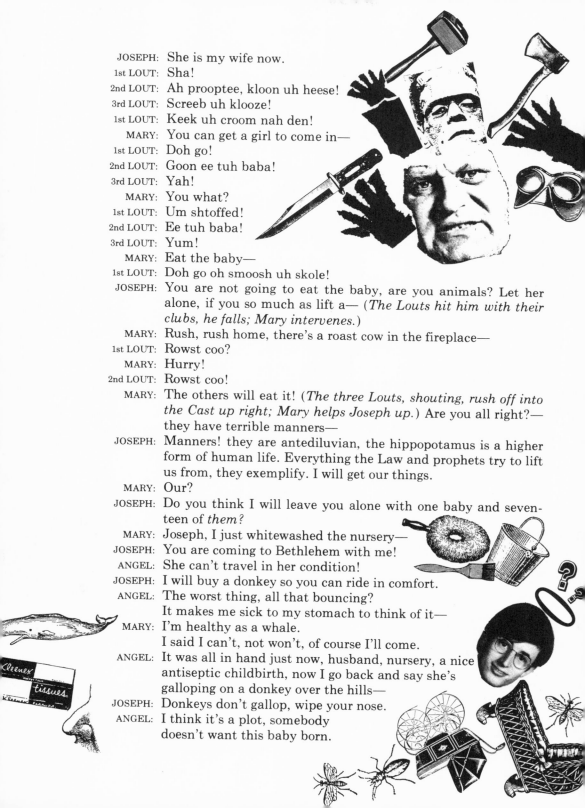

JOSEPH: She is my wife now.

1st LOUT: Sha!

2nd LOUT: Ah prooptee, kloon uh heese!

3rd LOUT: Screeb uh klooze!

1st LOUT: Keek uh croom nah den!

MARY: You can get a girl to come in—

1st LOUT: Doh go!

2nd LOUT: Goon ee tuh baba!

3rd LOUT: Yah!

MARY: You what?

1st LOUT: Um shtoffed!

2nd LOUT: Ee tuh baba!

3rd LOUT: Yum!

MARY: Eat the baby—

1st LOUT: Doh go oh smoosh uh skole!

JOSEPH: You are not going to eat the baby, are you animals? Let her alone, if you so much as lift a— (*The Louts hit him with their clubs, he falls; Mary intervenes.*)

MARY: Rush, rush home, there's a roast cow in the fireplace—

1st LOUT: Rowst coo?

MARY: Hurry!

2nd LOUT: Rowst coo!

MARY: The others will eat it! (*The three Louts, shouting, rush off into the Cast up right; Mary helps Joseph up.*) Are you all right?— they have terrible manners—

JOSEPH: Manners! they are antediluvian, the hippopotamus is a higher form of human life. Everything the Law and prophets try to lift us from, they exemplify. I will get our things.

MARY: Our?

JOSEPH: Do you think I will leave you alone with one baby and seventeen of *them?*

MARY: Joseph, I just whitewashed the nursery—

JOSEPH: You are coming to Bethlehem with me!

ANGEL: She can't travel in her condition!

JOSEPH: I will buy a donkey so you can ride in comfort.

ANGEL: The worst thing, all that bouncing?
It makes me sick to my stomach to think of it—

MARY: I'm healthy as a whale.
I said I can't, not won't, of course I'll come.

ANGEL: It was all in hand just now, husband, nursery, a nice antiseptic childbirth, now I go back and say she's galloping on a donkey over the hills—

JOSEPH: Donkeys don't gallop, wipe your nose.

ANGEL: I think it's a plot, somebody
doesn't want this baby born.

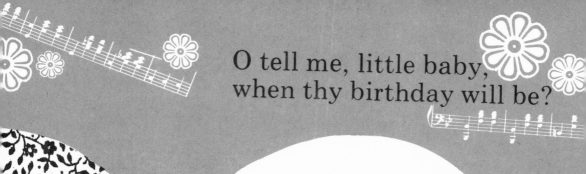

O tell me, little baby,
when thy birthday will be?

Ah, Joseph, you like him.

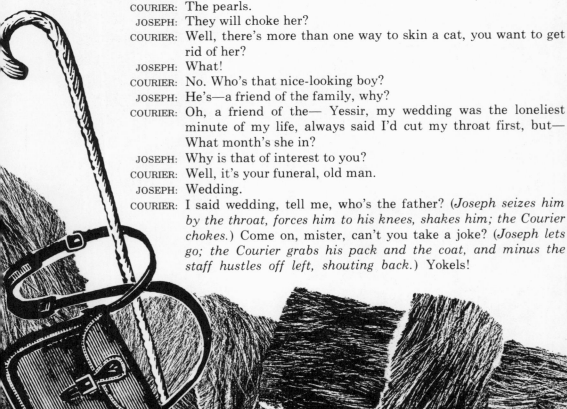

(*The Courier comes to them with his pack, staff, and the fur coat.*)

COURIER: Well, you're off to Bethlehem and me the other way, we may meet there. I see you're just married, how about a string of genuine maternity pearls for the bride, half-price so I don't have to carry them?

MARY: Joseph, save your money, we'll need it for the city, I hear prices turn your hair white in those cities.

COURIER: It is white, ho.

MARY: At least it's hair, how would you like what's left of yours pulled out?

COURIER: Oh?

MARY: I'll go get our things.

ANGEL: I'll go get a good safe donkey. (*Mary goes up left, the Angel up right into the cluster.*)

COURIER: Well, that's some bride you've got there, Joseph, full of beans. You want this choker?

JOSEPH: Choker?

COURIER: The pearls.

JOSEPH: They will choke her?

COURIER: Well, there's more than one way to skin a cat, you want to get rid of her?

JOSEPH: What!

COURIER: No. Who's that nice-looking boy?

JOSEPH: He's—a friend of the family, why?

COURIER: Oh, a friend of the— Yessir, my wedding was the loneliest minute of my life, always said I'd cut my throat first, but— What month's she in?

JOSEPH: Why is that of interest to you?

COURIER: Well, it's your funeral, old man.

JOSEPH: Wedding.

COURIER: I said wedding, tell me, who's the father? (*Joseph seizes him by the throat, forces him to his knees, shakes him; the Courier chokes.*) Come on, mister, can't you take a joke? (*Joseph lets go; the Courier grabs his pack and the coat, and minus the staff hustles off left, shouting back.*) Yokels!

(Mary returns without the veil, lugging a huge bag; Joseph hastens to take it, harsh.)

JOSEPH: Don't carry such things, are you an idiot?

MARY: What? *(Joseph lugs the bag down front.)* What's the matter?

JOSEPH: Nothing.

MARY: You're black as rain, Joseph.

JOSEPH: I want that nice-looking boy out of my sight!

MARY: Oh—

JOSEPH: Get him out of our lives or I'll smoosh his skole— *(He breaks off, appalled.)*

MARY: Joseph, you still say the nicest things, I thought with me so fat you wouldn't care.

JOSEPH: Oh Mary, Mary, every night I pray God to make me perfect and every morning in his infinite wisdom I wake up a putz, an old lunatic—

MARY: The best things are old, like cheese. Anyway, he's going back now— Hurry! *(This is to the Angel, who comes out of the cluster pulling a small and wobbly Donkey; he leads it to the bag, while Joseph stares.)*

JOSEPH: What species of quadruped is that?

ANGEL: It's a donkey, guaranteed not to gallop. Will you gallop? *(The Donkey shakes its head.)*

JOSEPH: The question is, will it live.

ANGEL: I'm sure it intends to live, don't you? *(The Donkey nods.)*

JOSEPH: Mary, you can't ride this sickly and stunted creature—

MARY: I'll walk.

ANGEL: It isn't stunted, it's immature.

MARY: I'll feed it, I'll build it up, it's more mature than my whole family—

JOSEPH: Mary.

MARY: Please!—we don't have time—

ANGEL: It's a farewell present, Joseph, I have to know she's safe.

MARY: See, it's taking his place.

JOSEPH: Oh, in that case we can rely on it. Very well, let's load it. *(He hoists the bag onto its back, the Donkey instantly collapses flat.)* Ha! a superlative animal but too spirited for you, Mary, promise you'll never ride him alone—

ANGEL: What's the matter with you?

DONKEY: *(weakly)* Carry me. Carry me.

ANGEL: You stop this nonsense and get up. Get up! Lift him up— (*They all lift the Donkey to its feet; Mary and Joseph turn away to repack the bag.*) You behave yourself, remember you're a beast of burden.

DONKEY: Why?

ANGEL: What?

DONKEY: Why am I a beast of burden?

ANGEL: I don't know, I—didn't make the world, it's your destiny, just be the best beast of burden in all the—

DONKEY: Bosh.

MARY: (*returns*) What?

ANGEL: He sneezed.

DONKEY: Pish and tush.

MARY: God bless you.

JOSEPH: (*straps bag on*) There. (*He picks up the staff, takes the halter from the Angel, and looks up; the others, including the Donkey, look up with him.*) God, we have a long journey, in your day and in your dark: be with us.

MARY: Be in us.

ANGEL: Be.

JOSEPH: To your mercy we confide these few belongings, which you have lent, and our lives, which you have lent, and especially the helpless new life which we carry with us we place in your care—

MARY: (*eyes closed*) In my care.

ANGEL: Care.

JOSEPH: —knowing that though we travel into a wilderness of wild beasts and bandits—

ANGEL: Bandits??

JOSEPH: —it is your wilderness, and we are in your hand. (*Facing out, he begins to walk in place, nods curtly to the Angel.*) Goodbye.

(*Facing out, Mary walks alongside the Donkey, the Angel retreating; she lifts her hand to him.*)

MARY: (*melancholy*) Goodbye, who'll take care of you?

ANGEL: I never thought of bandits!

MARY: Goodbye—goodbye, friend—

ANGEL: Wait! I'm coming with you! (*Joseph stops, the others stopping with him, and he turns to meet the Angel, grimly.*)

JOSEPH: If you are a nephew, join your dead uncle. If you are an angel, fly away. If you are the father of this child, say so.

ANGEL: I am not the father, you—woolheaded—

JOSEPH: (*roaring*) Then get out! (*The Angel falls back, unnerved. Joseph takes the halter again and they walk, Mary waving back as the Angel's feet retreat with him into the shadows. The lights dim into night, and on the rear wall a large star begins faintly to shine. They walk, and after a moment Mary begins sniffling; Joseph without looking hands her a handkerchief.*)

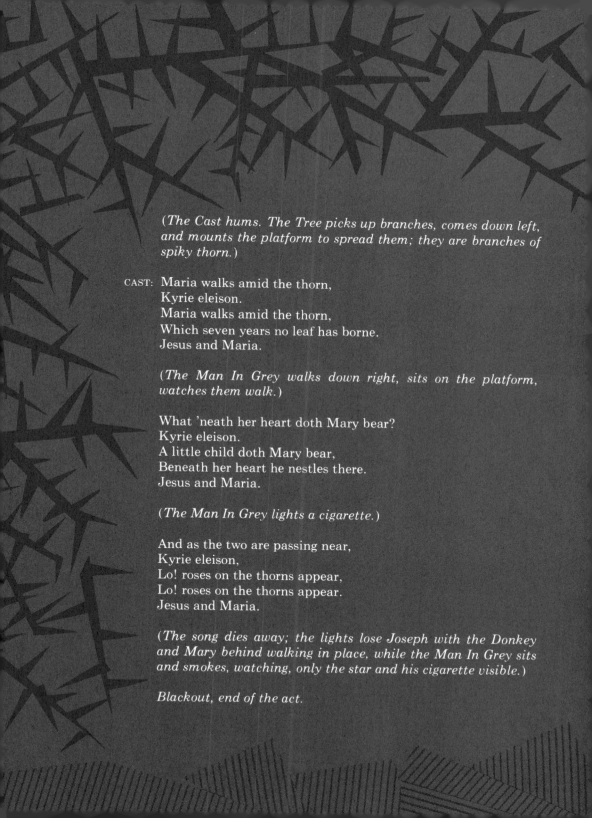

(*The Cast hums. The Tree picks up branches, comes down left, and mounts the platform to spread them; they are branches of spiky thorn.*)

CAST: Maria walks amid the thorn,
Kyrie eleison.
Maria walks amid the thorn,
Which seven years no leaf has borne.
Jesus and Maria.

(*The Man In Grey walks down right, sits on the platform, watches them walk.*)

What 'neath her heart doth Mary bear?
Kyrie eleison.
A little child doth Mary bear,
Beneath her heart he nestles there.
Jesus and Maria.

(*The Man In Grey lights a cigarette.*)

And as the two are passing near,
Kyrie eleison,
Lo! roses on the thorns appear,
Lo! roses on the thorns appear.
Jesus and Maria.

(*The song dies away; the lights lose Joseph with the Donkey and Mary behind walking in place, while the Man In Grey sits and smokes, watching, only the star and his cigarette visible.*)

Blackout, end of the act.

House lights on.

*The Cast take their places as at the close
of the first act; they sing.*

CAST: God rest you merry, gentlemen,
Let nothing you dismay;
Remember Christ our Savior
Was born on Christmas Day,
To save us all from Satan's power—
(*The Man In Grey passes among them.*)
When we were gone astray.
O tidings of comfort and joy, comfort and joy,
O tidings of comfort and joy.

Now to the Lord sing praises,
All you within this place,
And with true love and brotherhood
Each other now embrace—
(*They embrace.*)
This holy tide of Christmas
All other doth efface.
O tidings of comfort and joy, comfort and joy,
O tidings of comfort and joy.

House lights off, stage lights on.

It is night, and the star on the rear wall shines. The Tree stands on the platform left with her thorn branches; Joseph with his staff, the Donkey, and Mary at its side are walking in place, slowly.

JOSEPH: Are you tired, Mary?

MARY: Yes. I am tired these last days. (*Joseph stops the walk.*)

JOSEPH: I think we will camp tonight under this tree. (*He unloads the Donkey, who at once collapses on the ground asleep; Joseph takes a blanket from the bag, and food.*)

MARY: (*looking out right*) What are all those fireflies, Joseph?

JOSEPH: Bethlehem. Sit, I will make the fire.

MARY: Bethlehem. (*She sits on the platform right, wide-legged, holds her belly; Joseph collects as-if wood, and the Tree drops him a small branch. He looks at Mary as he makes the fire.*)

JOSEPH: Are you in pain, child?

MARY: No, I'm healthy as a whale.

JOSEPH: You miss that nice-looking boy.

MARY: No, I'm healthy as a whale.

JOSEPH: An absent-minded one.

MARY: No, I'm— What?

JOSEPH: Are you in love with him?

MARY: With who?

JOSEPH: That boy.

MARY: How did he get into the conversation? he's a *boy.*

JOSEPH: Yes.

MARY: I mean he's an angel, but a boy, I couldn't love anyone so immature. He doesn't inspire confidence.

JOSEPH: (*grim*) True.

MARY: That's a funny question, Joseph, you must be jealous of him.

JOSEPH: That is very observant of you.

MARY: Why?—it's weak men are jealous, you're so strong.

JOSEPH: Strong.

MARY: Yes.

JOSEPH: I inspire confidence.

MARY: Oh, yes.

JOSEPH: (*surprised*) Perhaps I'm strong. Well. Protein, vitamins, calcium, iron, everything two require, here. (*He brings her a bowl of food.*) Are you cold?—come to the fire—

MARY: No, I'm always warm from inside. Give me your hand. (*She guides it to her belly, and eats with her fingers; Joseph stands.*)

JOSEPH: (*starts*) Oh, dear God.

MARY: (*chewing*) Isn't it though?

JOSEPH: Oh, that's amazing.

MARY: Mm, he's company, like if it's cold I'm not cold and when I'm alone I'm not alone and if I die I'll go on living, I'm part of the whole human family, so now I don't think they're the horrible numskulls they are.

JOSEPH: He did it again!

MARY: And you're a good cook too. If I die you'll make him healthy things like this, Joseph, it's his favorite.

JOSEPH: Little whale, you are obsessed with dying tonight.

MARY: No, living, isn't it exciting now?

JOSEPH: Yes. Yes.

MARY: Of course *if* sometimes a mother dies the father has to be the mother, Joseph, and even if you're not the father you'd make a very good mother. It's what makes you so strong, what would I do without you? (*She gives him back the bowl.*) Only we're sleepy now. (*She waddles back to the bag and blanket; Joseph stares at the bowl.*)

JOSEPH: What indeed. (*He is moved, eats a handful from the bowl, knuckles at a tear, eats another handful, and looks up.*) Oh God, I thank you. (*After a moment he does a jig-skip with the bowl, and turns to Mary.*) I— (*But she is lying against the bag, her eyes closed; and he tiptoes around the Donkey to bend over her.*) Are you asleep, Mary? (*She doesn't answer, and he squats behind her, whispering.*) Then I will tell you. I am not the man either of us thinks, not so strong and not so weak, but all my life I have carried a child in me too, a deformed thing I've been ashamed of, with such—thoughts I turn my own eyes away, and you say come, come out, I need a whole man, and he —comes out, and for you I can perhaps be a whole man— (*He touches her belly with his fingertips; Mary takes his hand and he finds her eyes open upon him.*)

MARY: Kiss me, Joseph. (*Joseph blinks at her a moment, then kisses her on the mouth.*) So that's how it's done.

JOSEPH: Well, that is part of how it is done. I am not very—

MARY: Show me a little more of how it's done. (*Joseph kisses her again. The Tree is interested, her branches shiver, she loses one or two more.*) Ohhh. I don't know that it's so disappointing after all. (*Joseph stands up suddenly.*)

JOSEPH: Mary, Mary, go to sleep at once.

MARY: Where will you sleep?

JOSEPH: With the donkey.

MARY: Joseph you're a good, kind—honest man, and I— (*But she falls asleep, holding his hand. Joseph disengages it gently, tucks the blanket under her chin, puts the bowl away, rises again, steps over the Donkey, and curls up against it; he closes his eyes. The Donkey begins snoring.*)

JOSEPH: What, you snore too? (*He pokes the Donkey, who raises its head.*)

DONKEY: Uh?

JOSEPH: Stop snoring.
(*They lie down again, and all sleep.*)

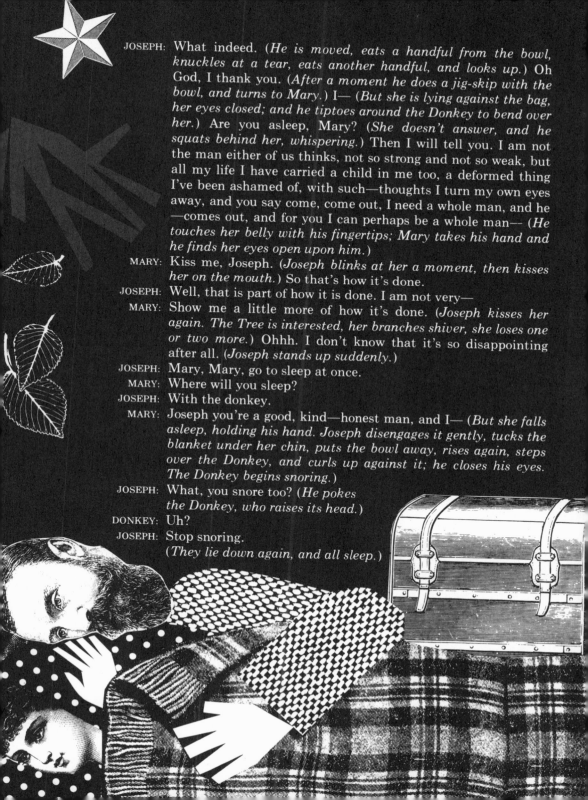

(The Man In Grey walks down left and stands beneath the Tree, gazing out at the night and at the sleepers.)

MAN IN GREY: Denizens of the dark. I love the dark.—But where is our angel?

TREE: Quit.

MAN IN GREY: Quit?

TREE: Fired.

MAN IN GREY: *(interested)* By whom?

TREE: Joseph.

MAN IN GREY: Oh. I thought superseded, by one of talent. No, he'll be back; it's his half of the story. In which he is to work a miracle.

TREE: Oh?

MAN IN GREY: And I unwork it.

TREE: That should be interesting.

MAN IN GREY: Not very. *(He puts his hand on the Tree's leg; her branches shiver.)* I have a favor to ask you.

TREE: *(shivering)* Go ahead.

MAN IN GREY: If I were to teach you what to say, and when, would you say it for me?

TREE: *(stops)* Is that all?

MAN IN GREY: It's very important.

TREE: Well, it depends.

MAN IN GREY: On what?

TREE: On how hard it is to say, some words have seven or four syllables.

MAY IN GREY: Yes.

TREE: Syl, la, bles, two's about my limit.

MAN IN GREY: It's a very simple word.

TREE: Go ahead.

MAN IN GREY: No.

TREE: Go ahead.

MAN IN GREY: The word is no.

TREE: Go ahead.

MAN IN GREY: Say it.

TREE: I'm trying! I have this speech problem, ever since I was fifteen, whenever I try to say—that word it comes out go ahead. That's how I got that beautiful bark.

MAN IN GREY: I see. Where is it?

TREE: The tax-collector took it.

MAN IN GREY: Would you like another, of black sable?

TREE: Black sable!

MAN IN GREY: Say no.

TREE: Yes!

MAN IN GREY: Say, no.

TREE: *(in pain)* Go ahead. I can't!

MAN IN GREY: Nuh.
        TREE: Nuh.
MAN IN GREY: Oh.
        TREE: Oh.
MAN IN GREY: No.
        TREE: No ahead.
MAN IN GREY: Leave out a—
        TREE: No head.
MAN IN GREY: Leave out ahead.
        TREE: No—No, I said it!
MAN IN GREY: Come. (*He hands her down,*
             turns her upstage left.) I must go
             into certain things more deeply—
        TREE: Go ahead.
MAN IN GREY: May I take your arms?
             (*He relieves her of the thorn branches,*
             as they go out.)

(From up right the three Kings, carrying their gift packages of gold, white, and black, enter; they sing in close harmony.)

KINGS: We three Kings of Orient are,
Bearing gifts we traverse afar
Field and fountain, moor and mountain,
Following yonder star.
Ohhhhhh
Star of wonder, star of night—
(The 1st King opens a road-map.)

1st KING: *(the dominant one)* I think we are here.

2nd KING: *(the timid one)* Where?

1st KING: At the junction of 7 and 20.

3rd KING: *(the dumb one)* I don't see us.

1st KING: We are not *on* the map, stupid, we are in the real world.

2nd KING: Are we lost, then?

1st KING: Yes and no. Yes until we get to the babe, then no.

3rd KING: How do we get to the babe?

1st KING: Look for the star!—west on 20, northwest on 72— *(They begin unfolding the map, which is endless.)* —east on 103, south on 204—

2nd KING: —west on 528?—

3rd KING: —east on 825—

1st KING: —southeast on 46, north on 219, south on 219, north on 219—

2nd KING: —west on 432?—

3rd KING: —east on 234—

1st KING: —northsouth on 219, and there we are.

3rd KING: Where?

1st KING: At the junction of 7 and 20, there is something wrong with this map. *(He gazes around, spots the sleepers.)* There is the star, but who are these characters?

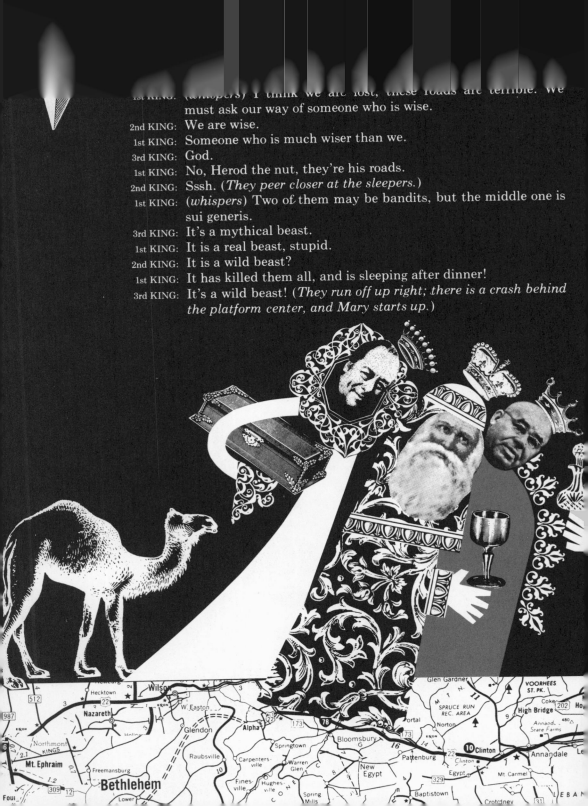

1st KING: (*whispers*) I think we are lost, these roads are terrible. We must ask our way of someone who is wise.
2nd KING: We are wise.
1st KING: Someone who is much wiser than we.
3rd KING: God.
1st KING: No, Herod the nut, they're his roads.
2nd KING: Sssh. (*They peer closer at the sleepers.*)
1st KING: (*whispers*) Two of them may be bandits, but the middle one is sui generis.
3rd KING: It's a mythical beast.
1st KING: It is a real beast, stupid.
2nd KING: It is a wild beast?
1st KING: It has killed them all, and is sleeping after dinner!
3rd KING: It's a wild beast! (*They run off up right; there is a crash behind the platform center, and Mary starts up.*)

MARY: Joseph, there's a wild beast—

JOSEPH: (*wakes*) A wild beast?

DONKEY: Wild beast? wild beast? (*Joseph runs with his staff up around the center platform right, the Angel runs down around it left.*)

ANGEL: There's a wild beast! (*He collides with Mary, drops the trumpet and promptbook, holds her; Joseph turns to see.*)

JOSEPH: You!

MARY: Oh, it's only you, how glad I am you've come—

JOSEPH: What am I seeing with my very eyes, a rendezvous?

ANGEL: I had to. I'm responsible for this baby—

JOSEPH: (*outraged*) While I sleep? (*He runs down with the staff to brain him, the Angel retreats, and Mary shakes a finger in Joseph's face.*)

MARY: Joseph, now I've had enough and it's too much, stop it! he came to help us, there's nobody else to look after him. What will make you believe him?

JOSEPH: A miracle.

ANGEL: (*with interest*) Really? What kind?

DONKEY: Sssssh! (*The Donkey sleeps again; Joseph marches away, leans on his staff, gazes glumly out; the Angel picks up the trumpet and promptbook. The lights begin to rise.*)

MARY: Did you eat?

ANGEL: No, my stomach's upset. I could change his staff to a snake—

MARY: Can you do that?

ANGEL: I never tried. (*He makes a dubious pass; Mary stops him.*)

MARY: He won't like it. What's wrong with your stomach?

ANGEL: I have a very nervous stomach.

MARY: It's nervous because you didn't eat, you have to set its mind at rest.

ANGEL: Will he really believe a miracle? (*He picks up the fallen branches, thinking; Mary rummages in the bag.*)

MARY: Here, we have some crusts and a bag of rice—

ANGEL: Do you have any strawberries?

MARY: What?

ANGEL: In the middle of the night I get this craving for strawberries. If I could—work a—

MARY: But it's practically sun-up, see?

ANGEL: Yes, then the morning comes and I'm— (*He sways, his tongue protrudes.*) —sick to my stommmach—

MARY: (*sees the star*) What is *that*?

ANGEL: (*sways*) Just some star, I see I'm going to have to work up a miracle. If I—live, that is—

MARY: (*alarmed*) Here, lie down, lie down. Joseph! (*She helps the Angel down with his head pillowed on the Donkey, who wakes again.*)

DONKEY: (*indignant*) Pleeease.

JOSEPH: (*unmoved*) What is the matter now?

MARY: He's very sick, come look how pale he is.

JOSEPH: It must be something he ate.

ANGEL: Ate!—aghhh—

MARY: Joseph, it may be ptomaine, we've got to get him to the doctor.

JOSEPH: What doctor?

MARY: In Bethlehem.

ANGEL: No, let me—die here—

JOSEPH: Let him die here.

MARY: Joseph! and you always such a good man. Donkey, get up!

JOSEPH: Always such a good man is wearing me out.

MARY: Both of you! *you* lie on *him*. (*The Angel falls athwart the Donkey, who belches; Mary shakes out the blanket.*) I'm disappointed in you, Joseph, you're making a big mistake.

JOSEPH: I do not know any doctors in Bethlehem!

ANGEL: There's an—obstetrician, I just came from Bethlehem—

MARY: (*covering his behind*) Don't talk, what were you doing in Bethlehem?

ANGEL: —for Joseph and—you, reservations—

MARY: For what?

ANGEL: —at the inn. I didn't want—anything to go wrong, I got the bridal suite.

MARY: I hope somebody not very far from this neighborhood who with his big suspicious ears isn't hard of hearing heard that. (*She hefts up the bag in her arms, fumbles for the Donkey's halter.*) Goodbye, Joseph, if you want me I'll be in the bridal suite with him.

JOSEPH: (*roars*) Drop that bag! (*Mary drops it in terror. The star is fading out, the lights growing. Joseph comes, loads the bag on his shoulder, takes the halter, and starts to back out tugging at the Donkey.*)

DONKEY: Help—

JOSEPH: This is the last trip I will make with this family! (*With the Donkey hanging back, the Angel draped over him, Joseph pulling in front and Mary pushing behind, they crawl off up right.*)

Glory to the
new-born Ki

(The cast sings.)

CAST: Hark! the herald angels sing,
"Glory to the new-born King!
Peace on earth, and mercy mild,
God and sinners reconciled!"
Joyful, all ye nations, rise,
Join the triumph of the skies,
With th' angelic hosts proclaim,
"Christ is born in Bethlehem!"
Hark! the herald angels sing,
"Glory to the new-born King!"

Joyful
all ye nations, rise—
triumph of the skie

(*Meanwhile from up left the two Women, now in rich shawls and bejewelled nose-veils, back in bowing fearfully; Herod follows—he is the Man In Grey but does not know it, harsh and fast-spoken, with a regal robe over his grey costume—driving them in a royal tantrum. The lights are up.*)

A Nut.

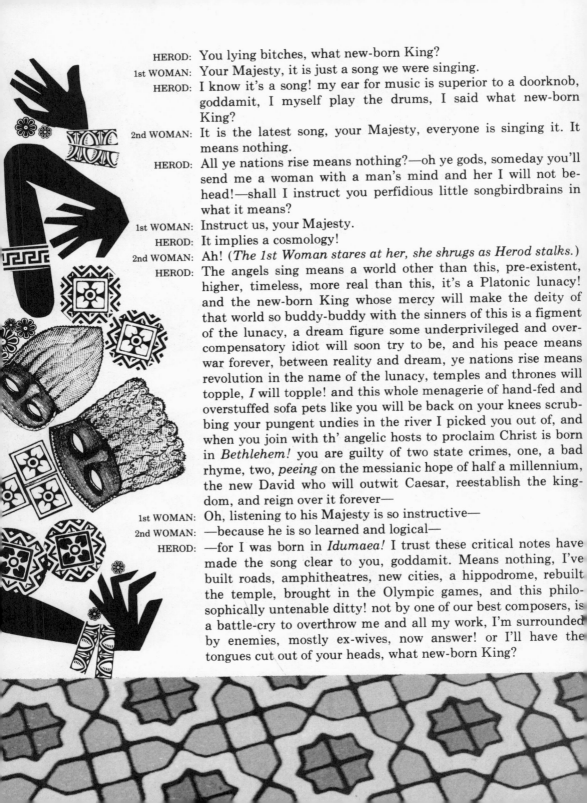

HEROD: You lying bitches, what new-born King?

1st WOMAN: Your Majesty, it is just a song we were singing.

HEROD: I know it's a song! my ear for music is superior to a doorknob, goddamit, I myself play the drums, I said what new-born King?

2nd WOMAN: It is the latest song, your Majesty, everyone is singing it. It means nothing.

HEROD: All ye nations rise means nothing?—oh ye gods, someday you'll send me a woman with a man's mind and her I will not behead!—shall I instruct you perfidious little songbirdbrains in what it means?

1st WOMAN: Instruct us, your Majesty.

HEROD: It implies a cosmology!

2nd WOMAN: Ah! (*The 1st Woman stares at her, she shrugs as Herod stalks.*)

HEROD: The angels sing means a world other than this, pre-existent, higher, timeless, more real than this, it's a Platonic lunacy! and the new-born King whose mercy will make the deity of that world so buddy-buddy with the sinners of this is a figment of the lunacy, a dream figure some underprivileged and over-compensatory idiot will soon try to be, and his peace means war forever, between reality and dream, ye nations rise means revolution in the name of the lunacy, temples and thrones will topple, *I* will topple! and this whole menagerie of hand-fed and overstuffed sofa pets like you will be back on your knees scrubbing your pungent undies in the river I picked you out of, and when you join with th' angelic hosts to proclaim Christ is born in *Bethlehem!* you are guilty of two state crimes, one, a bad rhyme, two, *peeing* on the messianic hope of half a millennium, the new David who will outwit Caesar, reestablish the kingdom, and reign over it forever—

1st WOMAN: Oh, listening to his Majesty is so instructive—

2nd WOMAN: —because he is so learned and logical—

HEROD: —for I was born in *Idumaea!* I trust these critical notes have made the song clear to you, goddamit. Means nothing, I've built roads, amphitheatres, new cities, a hippodrome, rebuilt the temple, brought in the Olympic games, and this philosophically untenable ditty! not by one of our best composers, is a battle-cry to overthrow me and all my work, I'm surrounded by enemies, mostly ex-wives, now answer! or I'll have the tongues cut out of your heads, what new-born King?

A Nut.

1st WOMAN: Your Majesty, it is just a song—

2nd WOMAN: Means nothing.

HEROD: Ye nations rise means nothing? oh ye gods— I said that, where *is* the mad assassin?

1st WOMAN: Which one?

HEROD: The goddam infant, where is he? what's his name? where can I ferret him out?

1st WOMAN: Your Majesty, there are three other Kings outside asking the same questions.

HEROD: I hope they're getting better answers.

2nd WOMAN: The song says Bethlehem, but—

HEROD: But?

2nd WOMAN: —not the address.

1st WOMAN: They say he is not born yet.

HEROD: In hiding, he's cleverer than the others, but I'll crush the little bastard in the snake's egg. Where is Bethlehem?

2nd WOMAN: (*points two ways*) It is an obscure town five miles to the south—

HEROD: Five miles!

2nd WOMAN: (*a third way*) To the south—

HEROD: Well! they think I have nothing better to do than risk a journey across five miles of wild beasts and ex-wives to an obscure town and personally look into every pregnant female jumping with germs? Send in the three Kings.

2nd WOMAN: Yes, your Majesty.

HEROD: And bring me my drums.

1st WOMAN: Yes, your Majesty.

HEROD: And tell the executioner to cut out your tongues.

2nd WOMAN: Yes, your Majesty. (*They bow out, up left.*)

(*The three Kings come down with their gift-packages.*)

HEROD: She will forget, I'm expected to remember everything myself. Welcome, royal friends!

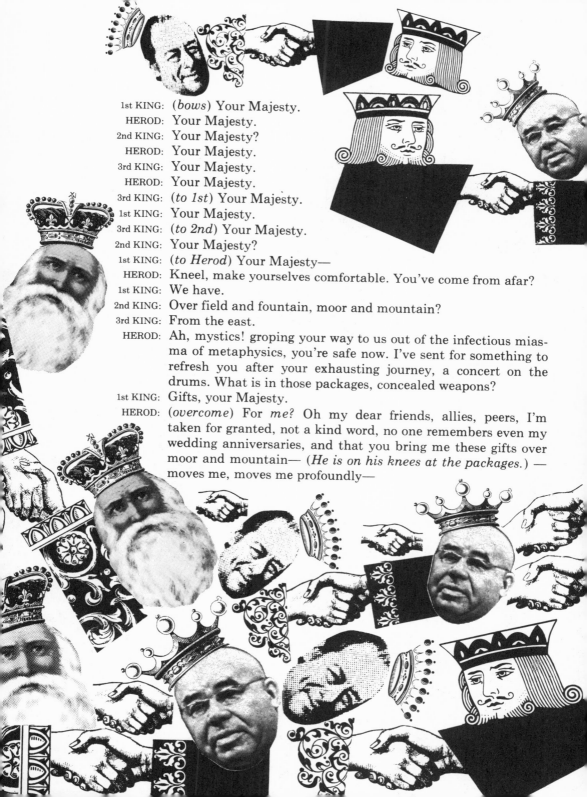

1st KING: (*bows*) Your Majesty.

HEROD: Your Majesty.

2nd KING: Your Majesty?

HEROD: Your Majesty.

3rd KING: Your Majesty.

HEROD: Your Majesty.

3rd KING: (*to 1st*) Your Majesty.

1st KING: Your Majesty.

3rd KING: (*to 2nd*) Your Majesty.

2nd KING: Your Majesty?

1st KING: (*to Herod*) Your Majesty—

HEROD: Kneel, make yourselves comfortable. You've come from afar?

1st KING: We have.

2nd KING: Over field and fountain, moor and mountain?

3rd KING: From the east.

HEROD: Ah, mystics! groping your way to us out of the infectious miasma of metaphysics, you're safe now. I've sent for something to refresh you after your exhausting journey, a concert on the drums. What is in those packages, concealed weapons?

1st KING: Gifts, your Majesty.

HEROD: (*overcome*) For *me*? Oh my dear friends, allies, peers, I'm taken for granted, not a kind word, no one remembers even my wedding anniversaries, and that you bring me these gifts over moor and mountain— (*He is on his knees at the packages.*) — moves me, moves me profoundly—

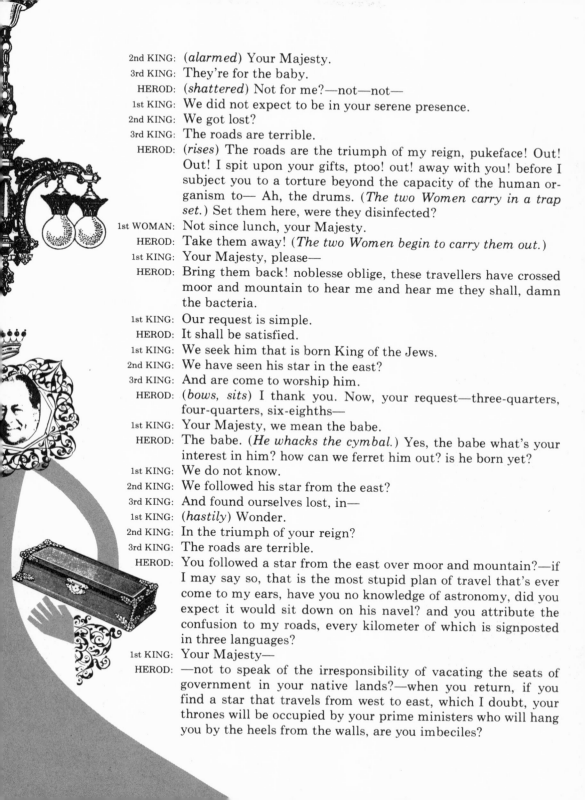

2nd KING: (*alarmed*) Your Majesty.

3rd KING: They're for the baby.

HEROD: (*shattered*) Not for me?—not—not—

1st KING: We did not expect to be in your serene presence.

2nd KING: We got lost?

3rd KING: The roads are terrible.

HEROD: (*rises*) The roads are the triumph of my reign, pukeface! Out! Out! I spit upon your gifts, ptoo! out! away with you! before I subject you to a torture beyond the capacity of the human organism to— Ah, the drums. (*The two Women carry in a trap set.*) Set them here, were they disinfected?

1st WOMAN: Not since lunch, your Majesty.

HEROD: Take them away! (*The two Women begin to carry them out.*)

1st KING: Your Majesty, please—

HEROD: Bring them back! noblesse oblige, these travellers have crossed moor and mountain to hear me and hear me they shall, damn the bacteria.

1st KING: Our request is simple.

HEROD: It shall be satisfied.

1st KING: We seek him that is born King of the Jews.

2nd KING: We have seen his star in the east?

3rd KING: And are come to worship him.

HEROD: (*bows, sits*) I thank you. Now, your request—three-quarters, four-quarters, six-eighths—

1st KING: Your Majesty, we mean the babe.

HEROD: The babe. (*He whacks the cymbal.*) Yes, the babe what's your interest in him? how can we ferret him out? is he born yet?

1st KING: We do not know.

2nd KING: We followed his star from the east?

3rd KING: And found ourselves lost, in—

1st KING: (*hastily*) Wonder.

2nd KING: In the triumph of your reign?

3rd KING: The roads are terrible.

HEROD: You followed a star from the east over moor and mountain?—if I may say so, that is the most stupid plan of travel that's ever come to my ears, have you no knowledge of astronomy, did you expect it would sit down on his navel? and you attribute the confusion to my roads, every kilometer of which is signposted in three languages?

1st KING: Your Majesty—

HEROD: —not to speak of the irresponsibility of vacating the seats of government in your native lands?—when you return, if you find a star that travels from west to east, which I doubt, your thrones will be occupied by your prime ministers who will hang you by the heels from the walls, are you imbeciles?

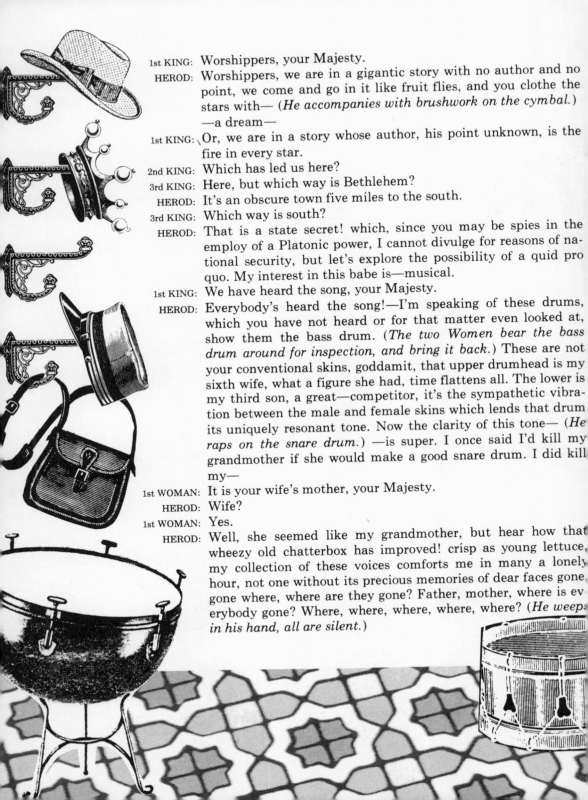

1st KING: Worshippers, your Majesty.

HEROD: Worshippers, we are in a gigantic story with no author and no point, we come and go in it like fruit flies, and you clothe the stars with— (*He accompanies with brushwork on the cymbal.*) —a dream—

1st KING: Or, we are in a story whose author, his point unknown, is the fire in every star.

2nd KING: Which has led us here?

3rd KING: Here, but which way is Bethlehem?

HEROD: It's an obscure town five miles to the south.

3rd KING: Which way is south?

HEROD: That is a state secret! which, since you may be spies in the employ of a Platonic power, I cannot divulge for reasons of national security, but let's explore the possibility of a quid pro quo. My interest in this babe is—musical.

1st KING: We have heard the song, your Majesty.

HEROD: Everybody's heard the song!—I'm speaking of these drums, which you have not heard or for that matter even looked at, show them the bass drum. (*The two Women bear the bass drum around for inspection, and bring it back.*) These are not your conventional skins, goddamit, that upper drumhead is my sixth wife, what a figure she had, time flattens all. The lower is my third son, a great—competitor, it's the sympathetic vibration between the male and female skins which lends that drum its uniquely resonant tone. Now the clarity of this tone— (*He raps on the snare drum.*) —is super. I once said I'd kill my grandmother if she would make a good snare drum. I did kill my—

1st WOMAN: It is your wife's mother, your Majesty.

HEROD: Wife?

1st WOMAN: Yes.

HEROD: Well, she seemed like my grandmother, but hear how that wheezy old chatterbox has improved! crisp as young lettuce, my collection of these voices comforts me in many a lonely hour, not one without its precious memories of dear faces gone, gone where, where are they gone? Father, mother, where is everybody gone? Where, where, where, where, where? (*He weeps in his hand, all are silent.*)

1st KING: Your Majesty, what has this to do with the babe?

HEROD: Drumheads are only human, they wear out, and in any case the silky skin of a new-born babe is a music I'm eager to hear, this one who threatens us all is—

1st KING: (*rising*) We must leave.

2nd KING: Oh yes, let's.

3rd KING: For the south, whichever—

HEROD: Stay, you haven't heard me play, we can kill two birds with one—

1st KING: Goodbye, your Majesty.

2nd KING: Hurry, get your package, stupid—

3rd KING: Oh, my package—

HEROD: (*rises*) Stay! I've perhaps aroused your suspicions, such was not my intent, no, I wish only that you search for the young child, and when you find him bring me word again—

1st KING: Why?

HEROD: (*cunningly*) That I may come and worship him also.

1st KING: I see.

HEROD: I rarely leave the palace, but so unusual a child—

1st KING: I see.

HEROD: You do see, now sit and I'll—Bring food and drink, you doodle-pates!— (*The two Women hurry out; Herod returns to the drums.*) —play you a funeral march I composed for the wealthy Sadducees I expropriated to finance the—where are you going!

1st KING: To find the babe.

HEROD: You will bring me word?

2nd KING: Oh, yes.

HEROD: Because if you don't!

3rd KING: What?

HEROD: I can have *all* the children killed, goddamit, a slaughter of the innocents, that won't look good on your record!

1st KING: Goodbye.

HEROD: Oh, but there's time, time, you haven't heard me play, time is what I create, nine-eighths, two-quarters, please stay— (*They bow and back out.*) Your word is my command, food, drink, women, boys? me?—please stay— (*But he is left talking to himself, forlorn.*) Please stay. Please stay.

kill—
—kill
kill!

A Nut.

—kill!

CAST: *(sings softly)* Silent night, holy night,
All is calm—
(But this carol we will not hear. Herod sits to attack the drums.)

HEROD: *(screaming)* Time is what I kill! and enemies, the earth is full of enemies and killers! rock, rock kills! and water kills! I have fire, fire kills! I have steel, steel kills! I have time, time kills, kills, kills, kills— *(He batters the drums in a frenzy, drowning himself out also.)*

(The lights have lost the Cast, still singing, but now with the star visible again they come down to strew the floor with armfuls of straw. Done, they carry the drums—and Herod also—off up right, which terminates his concert; we hear the carol's end.)

CAST: —tender and mild,
Sleep in heavenly peace,
Sleep in heavenly peace.

(*Joseph, led by the Girl with a candle, comes down left.*)

JOSEPH: This is a stable!

GIRL: Yes.

JOSEPH: But we have the bridal suite.

GIRL: It's all that's left, there's so many people to be taxed—

JOSEPH: Where are we to sleep, in the straw?

GIRL: It's nice in the straw,
there's a cute little mouse with big ears and eyes—

JOSEPH: (*pointing*)—and sheep urine and spiders and cowflops,
my wife is having a baby, not a mouse.

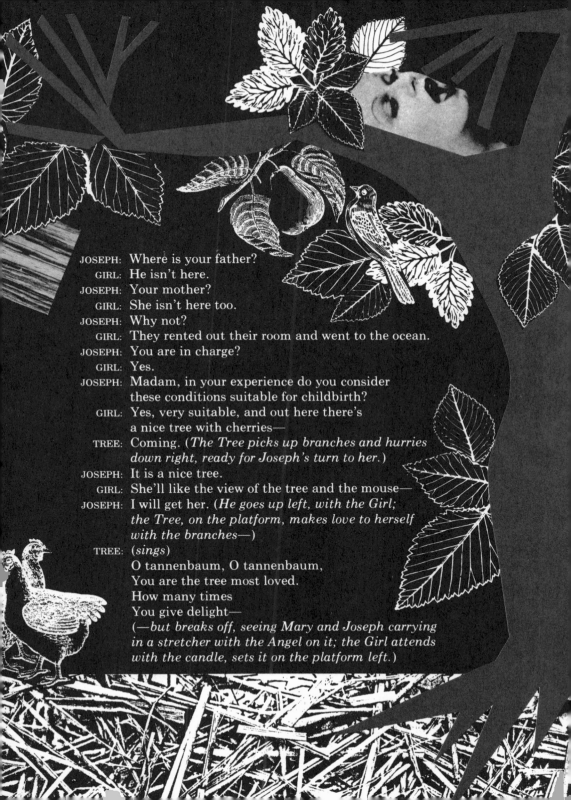

JOSEPH: Where is your father?

GIRL: He isn't here.

JOSEPH: Your mother?

GIRL: She isn't here too.

JOSEPH: Why not?

GIRL: They rented out their room and went to the ocean.

JOSEPH: You are in charge?

GIRL: Yes.

JOSEPH: Madam, in your experience do you consider
these conditions suitable for childbirth?

GIRL: Yes, very suitable, and out here there's
a nice tree with cherries—

TREE: Coming. (*The Tree picks up branches and hurries
down right, ready for Joseph's turn to her.*)

JOSEPH: It is a nice tree.

GIRL: She'll like the view of the tree and the mouse—

JOSEPH: I will get her. (*He goes up left, with the Girl;
the Tree, on the platform, makes love to herself
with the branches—*)

TREE: (*sings*)
O tannenbaum, O tannenbaum,
You are the tree most loved.
How many times
You give delight—
(*—but breaks off, seeing Mary and Joseph carrying
in a stretcher with the Angel on it; the Girl attends
with the candle, sets it on the platform left.*)

ANGEL: (*miserable*) It's my veins, I think the whole leg is swollen, does it look swollen?

MARY: No, which one?

ANGEL: The one that's bigger.

JOSEPH: They are both the same size.

ANGEL: They're both swollen, did you check my veins?

JOSEPH: When time permits I will gladly pull your veins out one by one and check them.

MARY: Joseph, that's not a nice thing to say to a sick angel, if you don't stop we're going to have to have a long talk.

JOSEPH: The ride is over, darling, off. (*He dumps the Angel onto the straw, picks up the stretcher.*) All I need on my hands now is a hypochondriacal angel— (*He takes the stretcher off up left; Mary gazes around.*)

MARY: And I just whitewashed the nursery.

ANGEL: Oh, Mary. You're not to carry heavy things, you ought to have an antiseptic place—

MARY: Well, to work again.

ANGEL: Why didn't your father say stable?

GIRL: He did.

ANGEL: He said bridal suite.

GIRL: It's where he keeps the bridles.

ANGEL: I spelled it wrong! how can I make so many mistakes?

MARY: (*exploring*) Anybody can make a mistake, it's human.

ANGEL: Human?

MARY: Of course.

ANGEL: Oh, I'm even lowering your standards.

MARY: (*back of the platform center*) I'll have him here. Now. Are you an efficient little girl?

GIRL: Yes, very efficient.

MARY: Good. I want a rake, a broom, a mop, a bucket of hot water, soap, a pair of sheets, sterilized scissors, some string, and two armfuls of clean rags, and I want them fast.

GIRL: Yes, ma'am. (*She hurries out, left.*)

MARY: You rest.

ANGEL: Mary, you're coming through this better than me—

MARY: It's all in your head, rest your head. (*She goes waddling out after the Girl; the Angel clutches his abdomen.*)

TREE: What happened to you?
ANGEL: I thought it was varicose veins,
        but it seems to be cramps—
TREE: Oh, cramps.
ANGEL: —spots before the eyes—
TREE: Spots.
ANGEL: —chills and fever—
TREE: Chills and—
ANGEL: —hemorrhoids—
TREE: Well, I guess it's curtains
        for one bossy little angel.
ANGEL: —and I'm in no condition
        to work a miracle.
        Do you have a pickle?
TREE: Do I look like a pickle tree?
ANGEL: And a ringing in my ears,
        I keep hearing—music—
TREE: Me too.

(*The Cast in darkness sings softly, the Angel cupping his ear;
The Tree makes love to herself with the branches.*)

CAST: Then Mary spoke to Joseph,
So sweet and so mild,
"Joseph, gather me some cherries,
For I am with child,
Joseph, gather me some cherries—"

ANGEL: Is that what you hear?
TREE: Is what what I hear?
ANGEL: What I hear.

CAST: Then Joseph flew in anger,
In anger flew he,
"Let the father of the baby
Gather cherries for thee—"

TREE: How do I know if it's what I hear if I don't hear it?
ANGEL: Let the father of the baby—It's a song about a miracle—
TREE: I hear my song. (*She sings.*)
O tannenbaum, O tannenbaum,
Your leaves are ever faithful.
Not only—
(*She inspects her leaves.*) What kind of tree am I this time?
ANGEL: (*inattentive*) Cherry.
TREE: Then how come I've got pears? You call that faithful?
ANGEL: (*attentive*) Cherry?
TREE: Can't you get anything right?
ANGEL: Cherries, I'll get you cherries! (*He snatches the pear branches;
the Cast sings while the Angel exchanges them for cherry
branches, and returns to the Tree.*)

CAST: The cherry tree bowed low down,
Bowed low down to the ground—
ANGEL: There. Now if you bow low down for Joseph—

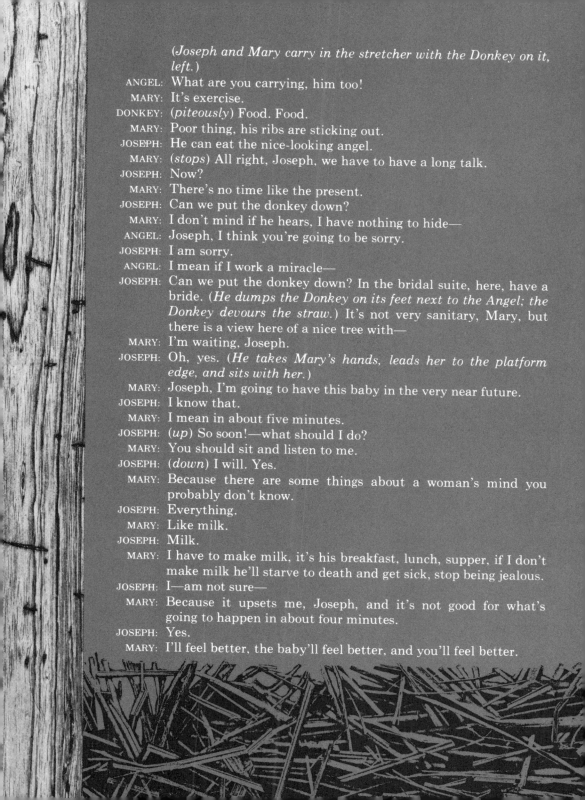

(*Joseph and Mary carry in the stretcher with the Donkey on it, left.*)

ANGEL: What are you carrying, him too!

MARY: It's exercise.

DONKEY: (*piteously*) Food. Food.

MARY: Poor thing, his ribs are sticking out.

JOSEPH: He can eat the nice-looking angel.

MARY: (*stops*) All right, Joseph, we have to have a long talk.

JOSEPH: Now?

MARY: There's no time like the present.

JOSEPH: Can we put the donkey down?

MARY: I don't mind if he hears, I have nothing to hide—

ANGEL: Joseph, I think you're going to be sorry.

JOSEPH: I am sorry.

ANGEL: I mean if I work a miracle—

JOSEPH: Can we put the donkey down? In the bridal suite, here, have a bride. (*He dumps the Donkey on its feet next to the Angel; the Donkey devours the straw.*) It's not very sanitary, Mary, but there is a view here of a nice tree with—

MARY: I'm waiting, Joseph.

JOSEPH: Oh, yes. (*He takes Mary's hands, leads her to the platform edge, and sits with her.*)

MARY: Joseph, I'm going to have this baby in the very near future.

JOSEPH: I know that.

MARY: I mean in about five minutes.

JOSEPH: (*up*) So soon!—what should I do?

MARY: You should sit and listen to me.

JOSEPH: (*down*) I will. Yes.

MARY: Because there are some things about a woman's mind you probably don't know.

JOSEPH: Everything.

MARY: Like milk.

JOSEPH: Milk.

MARY: I have to make milk, it's his breakfast, lunch, supper, if I don't make milk he'll starve to death and get sick, stop being jealous.

JOSEPH: I—am not sure—

MARY: Because it upsets me, Joseph, and it's not good for what's going to happen in about four minutes.

JOSEPH: Yes.

MARY: I'll feel better, the baby'll feel better, and you'll feel better.

JOSEPH: I will do my best.

MARY: And that sick boy'll feel better, anyway you have no reason to be jealous, it isn't him I love, it's you.

JOSEPH: I will do my— (*He stops, halfway up.*) What?

MARY: What what?

JOSEPH: What is the last thing you said?

MARY: It isn't him I love, it's you.

JOSEPH: (*stammering*) Why, why—Why didn't you say so?

MARY: I did.

JOSEPH: You didn't.

MARY: I didn't but I do.

JOSEPH: You never said so.

MARY: I did say so.

JOSEPH: No.

MARY: I did, when you kissed me, I said you're a good honest man and I love you.

JOSEPH: No.

MARY: I did.

JOSEPH: No. You fell asleep.

MARY: Well, I don't change just because I fall asleep, I love you when I'm asleep too.

JOSEPH: (*sits*) I feel weak.

MARY: Everyone is feeling weak and I'm having the baby. I need you, Joseph, there's a lot to do—

JOSEPH: Yes, yes. Mary, I will never, never be jealous again.
(*The Girl hurries in with a rake, broom, mop, bucket, sheets, scissors, rags.*)

GIRL: Is there anything else you want fast?

MARY: (*up*) Yes, a helping hand, because I—don't have much time now—

JOSEPH: (*up*) Now, is it now?

MARY: Soon.

ANGEL: Oh, what cramps! Where is the obstetrician?

GIRL: He rented out his office and went to the ocean.

ANGEL: Oh, no.

MARY: (*hands out things*) Joseph, rake. You sweep up after him. I'll mop because you won't get in the corners, and *you* rest and stop worrying, there won't be a crack with a germ left in it.
(*Joseph, the Girl, Mary go to work in the rear shadows; the lights narrow down to the Angel and the chewing Donkey.*)

ANGEL: You're eating my sickbed. (*He pulls straw away, the Donkey growls ferociously, the Angel drops it; he leafs through the promptbook.*) Not a word of guidance. (*He kneels up, looking into the lights; the star is bright behind him.*)

God? I'm confused, I have this miracle—but it's fraudulent and—

This child must be born, but who's to *keep* him alive? this man you chose disbelieves! and I want to get it right and come back, I'm juggling in the dark, alone, nobody answers my questions, and that they sent *me* is enough to make *me* disbelieve, are you there or not?—I couldn't even play the trumpet for him, see? (*He blows it fiercely, a wretched sound; and from up right the Man In Grey comes down.*) So what am I to do?

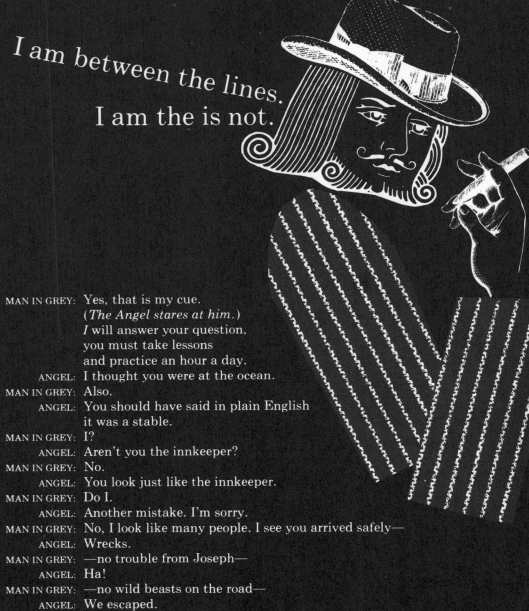

I am between the lines.
I am the is not.

MAN IN GREY:	Yes, that is my cue.
	(*The Angel stares at him.*)
	I will answer your question,
	you must take lessons
	and practice an hour a day.
ANGEL:	I thought you were at the ocean.
MAN IN GREY:	Also.
ANGEL:	You should have said in plain English
	it was a stable.
MAN IN GREY:	I?
ANGEL:	Aren't you the innkeeper?
MAN IN GREY:	No.
ANGEL:	You look just like the innkeeper.
MAN IN GREY:	Do I.
ANGEL:	Another mistake. I'm sorry.
MAN IN GREY:	No, I look like many people. I see you arrived safely—
ANGEL:	Wrecks.
MAN IN GREY:	—no trouble from Joseph—
ANGEL:	Ha!
MAN IN GREY:	—no wild beasts on the road—
ANGEL:	We escaped.
MAN IN GREY:	—and are bedded down to await this event in the hay,
	with I suppose no hope of infection—
ANGEL:	Well, they're cleaning—
MAN IN GREY:	—and time now to trump up a little miracle.
ANGEL:	What?
MAN IN GREY:	To convince Joseph. Your conscience is bothering you,
	of course, you'd prefer a genuine one, but none will happen;
	surely we are beyond that naiveté.

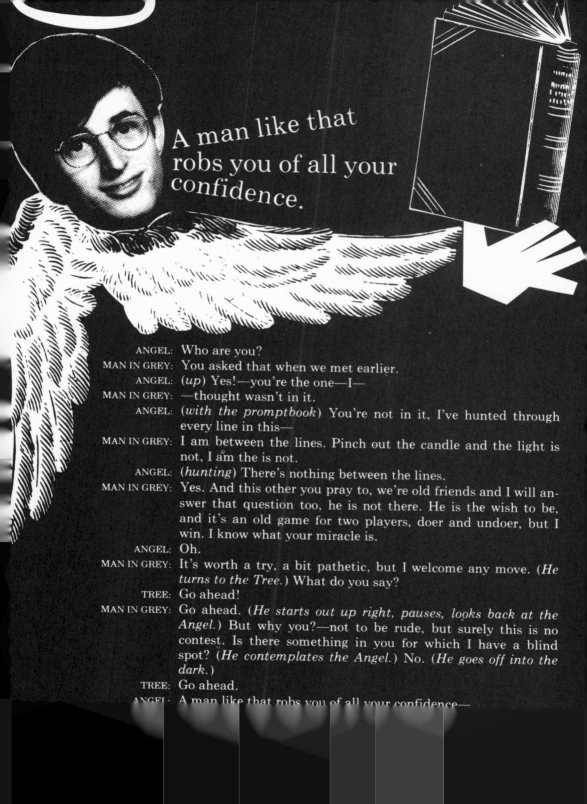

A man like that robs you of all your confidence.

ANGEL: Who are you?

MAN IN GREY: You asked that when we met earlier.

ANGEL: (*up*) Yes!—you're the one—I—

MAN IN GREY: —thought wasn't in it.

ANGEL: (*with the promptbook*) You're not in it, I've hunted through every line in this—

MAN IN GREY: I am between the lines. Pinch out the candle and the light is not, I am the is not.

ANGEL: (*hunting*) There's nothing between the lines.

MAN IN GREY: Yes. And this other you pray to, we're old friends and I will answer that question too, he is not there. He is the wish to be, and it's an old game for two players, doer and undoer, but I win. I know what your miracle is.

ANGEL: Oh.

MAN IN GREY: It's worth a try, a bit pathetic, but I welcome any move. (*He turns to the Tree.*) What do you say?

TREE: Go ahead!

MAN IN GREY: Go ahead. (*He starts out up right, pauses, looks back at the Angel.*) But why you?—not to be rude, but surely this is no contest. Is there something in you for which I have a blind spot? (*He contemplates the Angel.*) No. (*He goes off into the dark.*)

TREE: Go ahead.

ANGEL: A man like that robs you of all your confidence—

(*From the rear Mary with the broom shoos downstage the Cow and the Sheep; Joseph and the Girl, with rake and mop in bucket, follow.*)

MARY: Out, out, you can come back later. (*The Cow and the Sheep trot down right, sit by the Tree, and watch.*) Boil the pot and bring it back full, I'd like you with me. And— (*She leans on the platform, breathing.*) Aahh.

JOSEPH: I will be with you.

MARY: (*grittily*) Not—till I call—

ANGEL: Where is the obstetrician!

JOSEPH: At the ocean, with her father.

GIRL: He is my father.

ANGEL: What!

MARY: Boil the pot and don't watch it!—hurry— (*She hangs onto the platform, the Girl runs out left with the things, the Angel turns up after the Man In Grey, Joseph zigzags between Mary and the Girl.*)

JOSEPH: What shall I—Hurry!—do, shall I—

ANGEL: The obstetrician is the innkeeper is the—*Hope* of infection?

JOSEPH: Mary, lie down, nothing like this—Hurry!—has ever hap-

ANGEL: pened to me—
ANGEL: (*back*) Happened to you!
JOSEPH: Boil the pot!
ANGEL: Boil your father!
JOSEPH: Don't shout!
ANGEL: Be calm!
JOSEPH: Wipe your nose!
ANGEL: Don't shout!
JOSEPH: Be calm!
(*The Donkey wakes up—*)
DONKEY: Ssssh! (*—and lies down again, with Joseph and the Angel clutching each other; Mary straightens up.*)
MARY: Not this time. The donkey makes more sense than either of you. I can have a baby like any other animal, just be quiet and wait.
JOSEPH: Mary, dear child—
MARY: No, be quiet. Now sit down, both of you. Close your eyes. Put your hands on your knees, put your head on your hands. Now wait, till I call. (*Leaving them so on either side of the Donkey, Mary goes heavily around the platform center, and lies down behind it.*)

TREE: Well, what's the miracle?
ANGEL: (*gesturing*) Sssh. Not in front of—
JOSEPH: (*to him*) Be quiet, and wait.
ANGEL: (*to her*) Be quiet, and wait.
TREE: Be quiet, and wait.
(*She shrugs, and eats her own cherries.*)

(*The three Kings back on with their
gift-packages from the star up right,
turn to the group.*)
3rd KING: Are we in the right place?
1st KING: Where is he that is born King of the Jews?
ANGEL: Join us.
2nd KING: We have come to worship him?
ANGEL: Yes. Be quiet, and wait.

(*The Girl runs in with the bucket full,
disappears behind the platform center;
they stare.*)
MARY: (*off*) Joseph!
(*Joseph starts up, gazes wildly at them,
and runs back of the platform;
the others sit in silence, apprehensive.*)

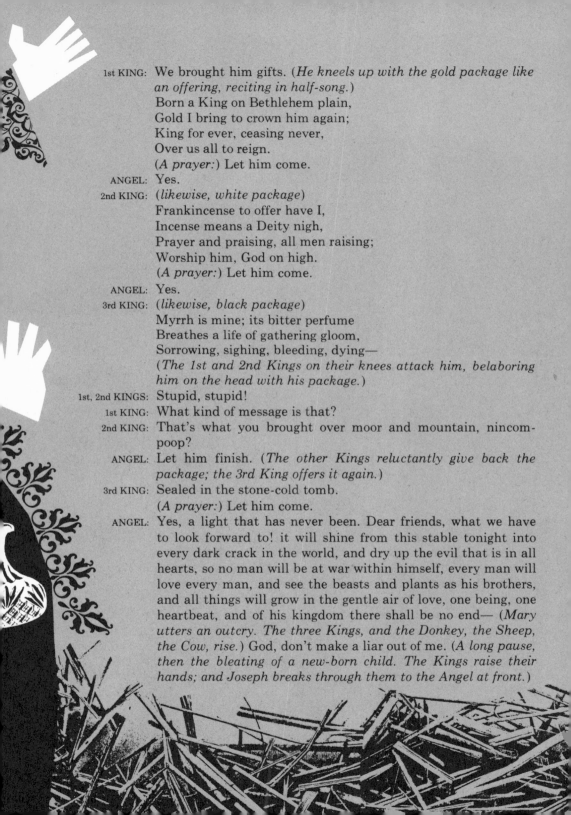

1st KING: We brought him gifts. (*He kneels up with the gold package like an offering, reciting in half-song.*)
Born a King on Bethlehem plain,
Gold I bring to crown him again;
King for ever, ceasing never,
Over us all to reign.
(*A prayer:*) Let him come.

ANGEL: Yes.

2nd KING: (*likewise, white package*)
Frankincense to offer have I,
Incense means a Deity nigh,
Prayer and praising, all men raising;
Worship him, God on high.
(*A prayer:*) Let him come.

ANGEL: Yes.

3rd KING: (*likewise, black package*)
Myrrh is mine; its bitter perfume
Breathes a life of gathering gloom,
Sorrowing, sighing, bleeding, dying—
(*The 1st and 2nd Kings on their knees attack him, belaboring him on the head with his package.*)

1st, 2nd KINGS: Stupid, stupid!

1st KING: What kind of message is that?

2nd KING: That's what you brought over moor and mountain, nincompoop?

ANGEL: Let him finish. (*The other Kings reluctantly give back the package; the 3rd King offers it again.*)

3rd KING: Sealed in the stone-cold tomb.
(*A prayer:*) Let him come.

ANGEL: Yes, a light that has never been. Dear friends, what we have to look forward to! it will shine from this stable tonight into every dark crack in the world, and dry up the evil that is in all hearts, so no man will be at war within himself, every man will love every man, and see the beasts and plants as his brothers, and all things will grow in the gentle air of love, one being, one heartbeat, and of his kingdom there shall be no end— (*Mary utters an outcry. The three Kings, and the Donkey, the Sheep, the Cow, rise.*) God, don't make a liar out of me. (*A long pause, then the bleating of a new-born child. The Kings raise their hands; and Joseph breaks through them to the Angel at front.*)

JOSEPH: It's a boy! (*The Angel faints; a King catches him. Joseph shakes hands with the other two.*) It's a boy! It's a boy! (*He runs back. The Donkey, the Cow, and the Sheep break into jubilant song.*)

DONKEY, COW, SHEEP: Adeste fideles, laeti triumphantes,
Venite, venite in Bethlehem!
(*Upright, they dance with each other.*)
Natum videte, regem angelorum,
Venite adoremus, venite adoremus—
(*The Angel revives, and with the Kings joins in the singing; they dance with the Donkey, the Cow, and the Sheep, passing each other from hand to hand.*)
—venite adoremus, Dominum.
Natum videte, regem angelorum,
Venite adoremus—

(*The dance builds; its climax depends on the set. If a burlap screen is employed, it is drawn back by Joseph to reveal a creche scene, Mary bent over a manger with its light bathing her face; the following dialog is cut to the trumpet fanfare. If only the center platform is employed, Mary comes unsteadily from behind it to stop the dance.*)

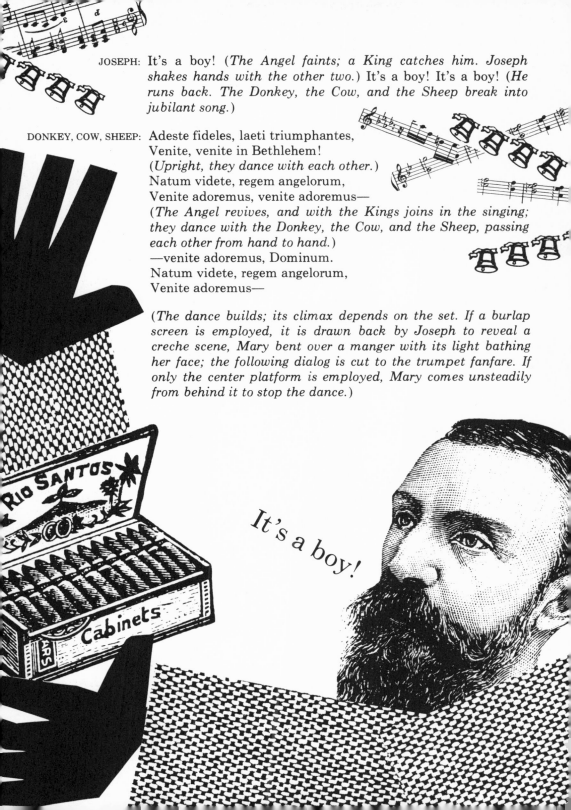

MARY: He looks just like— (*She changes her mind.*) There's only one word to describe him, indescribable. He's a perfectly normal baby in every respect—

(*A trumpet fanfare interrupts them; Herod rises in a light rear, his palm raised to greet unseen auditors.*)

Operation
Slaughter of the Innocents—
Loyal soldiers, I send you forth
Kill every female big with child
Kill every child!
Thank you.

OD: Treachery, treachery, once again treachery!—they did not bring me word. Loyal soldiers of the loyal throne, I send you forth as defenders of your homes, your God, your country: level that obscure town!—Operation Slaughter of the Innocents, kill every child, kill every female big with child, kill every woman who shields her child! but kill *the* child! Thank you.

(*The light dies on Herod, and in the dark a clanging of swords and neighing of horses rise; the stable is dim with the candle.*)

MARY: What, what?

1st KING: It is Herod, take the child and flee!

MARY: What, what? (*The 3rd Girl runs in from rear—*)

GIRL: Flee! (*—and runs out left; the Donkey, the Sheep, the Cow run in panic here and there.*)

JOSEPH: I'll get the child! (*He runs back.*)

2nd KING: Flee!

MARY: What?

3rd KING: Flee!

MARY: Where?

1st KING: Egypt! (*The three Kings scatter into the dark, with the Sheep and the Cow after them, and Mary runs back; the Donkey lies down and covers its head.*)

(*The Angel turns on the Tree, who is wind-shaken—the Cast is the wind, moaning.*)

ANGEL: Stand in place! (*The Tree spreads her shaking branches.*) It's very simple, when I say now! you bend and offer her cherries—

(*Joseph comes from behind the platform, Mary clinging to him; he fights her off, lunges at the Angel, and seizes him by the throat; the Angel falls to his knees, and Mary throws herself on Joseph.*)

JOSEPH: You are the father!

ANGEL: I'm not—

JOSEPH: You are the father! he looks like you!

MARY: Joseph—

JOSEPH: He looks exactly like you!

MARY: I need you, Joseph—

JOSEPH: What am I, a cat's-paw for the two of you, a comical old—

MARY: Get the child! let him go and—

JOSEPH: His child? his child? (*He chokes the Angel; Mary beats at his face, he lets go; she drags at his hands.*)

MARY: Come help me, we'll take the child and— (*Joseph throws her off, she falls.*)

JOSEPH: Let the child die!

MARY: (*a silence*) What?

ANGEL: Listen. (*In the silence a faint clatter of hooves is audible, growing; the wind rises.*) Soldiers.

MARY: Joseph!

JOSEPH: Let the child die! what is it to me if his child dies? (*He stumbles to the platform left, falls upon it at the candle.*) —or he dies, or you die, or I die?— (*He strikes with his fist.*) —nothing, it is all nothing— (*He puts his face on his fists; Mary comes on her knees behind him.*)

MARY: Say yes, Joseph, oh you're making a terrible mistake, I told you the truth but— It doesn't matter, it doesn't even matter I love you—

JOSEPH: Love.

MARY: —what else is there? only life, and nothing matters except love, I mean life, I mean love, I'm mixed up because I'm—hearing those horses! and whatever I mean *that's* the opposite! Say yes, what difference does it make whose child, yours, mine, his, it's alive, it's alive, say yes to it, did we come with it all this way to see it die? Help me, Joseph, Egypt, my God, I can't do this alone, say yes to it—I'm not going to see this child die—

ANGEL: Say Joseph, gather me some cherries.

MARY: Joseph, gather me some cherries— What!

JOSEPH: (*raging*) Let the father of the baby gather cherries for you!

ANGEL: (*turns*) Now. (*The Tree is rigid.*) Now!

TREE: Nuh oh. Nuh oh.

ANGEL: Stop everything! Lights! (*The hoofbeats and the wind break off, Joseph and Mary are arrested in mid-gesture, the Donkey raises its head; the lights jump.*) What do you mean, nuh oh?

TREE: Nuh oh, no. I said it!

ANGEL: This is the miracle, the climax of the story!

TREE: (*tries different ways*) No. No? No! No?! Nohhh—

ANGEL: Stop saying no! You think this is some half-baked modern work of existential negativism? it's affirmative!—a much-told tale, it can only end one way, yes—

TREE: What do I care how it ends, I made other arrangements.

ANGEL: With who?

TREE: None of your business, but I have a better idea. You need a miracle here?

ANGEL: Of course!

TREE: Change places with me.

ANGEL: What?

TREE: You be a tree! I never asked to be a tree, standing on this thing all night, I'm sick of it!

ANGEL: Change—places with—

TREE: I want to be a dancer!

ANGEL: I am the angel of the Lord. (*The wind begins to moan again, the lights dim.*) And must go back—

TREE: Oh no, you be a tree it's for keeps, no refunds, roots and all! because I've had it, you can stand here and offer her cherries forever—

ANGEL: Not go back? (*The Cast lifts from wind-sound to song—*)

CAST: The cherry tree bowed low down,
Bowed low down to the ground— (*but is joined by the clatter of hoofbeats, rising, close at hand; Joseph lifts his head.*)

TREE: (*the hoofbeats*) You hear?

ANGEL: Yes.

TREE: All this bull about one being, one heartbeat, yes or no?

JOSEPH: Oh God, give me a sign!

ANGEL: Oh God, give me a sign! (*They wait, separately, in vain.*)

TREE: Come on, you're a big boy now, you're on your own.

ANGEL: (*forlornly*) God?—

TREE: Make up your own mind.

This is
the miracle
climax
of the story!

ANGEL: —goodbye. Give me the branches. (*The Tree jumps down, and the Angel mounts the platform with the branches; she runs out.*)

TREE: Free!

(*Joseph rounds on Mary again—*)

JOSEPH: (*raging*) Let the father of the baby— (*and sees the Angel bowing with his branches of cherries, low and most graciously, to a sound of sanctuary bells*) —gather—cherries for— (*Joseph drops to his knees.*) Oh God, what have I almost done! have mercy on me, have mercy on me—

MARY: Help me! (*She runs back, Joseph after her; the hoofbeats are at hand, and are drowned out by voices screaming in terror.*)

(*The Donkey jumps up; the Angel as Tree is now upright.*)

(*Mary runs down with the baby bundled at her breast, followed by Joseph with the staff and the huge bag; he catches at the Donkey's halter, leads him down center.*)

JOSEPH: Come!

MARY: (*frantic*) Where is the angel, where is the angel?

JOSEPH: Come! (*He runs back and pulls Mary after him; they and the Donkey flatten out of sight on the lower floor, front.*)

(*In the shadows upstage the figures of all the others dart back and forth, screaming, pursued by a pair of Soldiers with swords, striking in the dark; bodies fall, crawl a bit, and are still.*)

(*The Tree in her fur coat staggers in left, inspects a sleeve in the light.*)

TREE: (*vexed*) This isn't black sable, it's the same coat! (*She falls, crawls, is still.*)

(Now the Man in Grey comes in swiftly at right, crossing to the candle, raises it, moves from left to right with it, staring out over the hidden family, and cannot find them; but he sees the Angel rigid as Tree.)

MAN IN GREY: Some—blind spot—

(At left the Girl and two other Children run into the light, and the Girl picks up the trumpet; turning then they see the Man In Grey, and freeze, exactly as before.)

MAN IN GREY: Well, again. *(He puts his hand out as for the trumpet; they back away down left, in a terrified huddle. The Man smiles at them. Then he lifts his hand in a sudden gesture; they begin screaming, blood trickles out of the mouth of one, the hand of another finds blood at her heart; all three fall and lie still.)* Now give me a kiss, and take your things home.

(He pinches out the candle.)

For the dark is real, and injustice is real and tears are real, and the dissolution of all things is real, and nothing else.

(A Soldier comes down right with a sword.)

SOLDIER: This is the tree, shall I hack it down?
MAN IN GREY: No. Let it grow, it will make a good cross, some day.
(They go out.)

(*A light begins to come up on Joseph, the Donkey, and Mary with the baby at her breast, as they rise and walk in place, front center.*)

(*The Cast, scattered in the dark onstage, sings— it begins dirge-like.*)

CAST: O little town of Bethlehem,
How still we see thee lie.
Above thy deep and dreamless sleep
The silent stars go by.
(*They begin to rise, kneeling.*)
Yet in thy dark streets shineth
The everlasting Light;
The hopes and fears of all the years
Are met in thee tonight.

(*They repeat, very softly, under the dialogue.*)
Yet in thy dark streets shineth
The everlasting Light;
Yet in thy dark streets shineth—

MARY: Egypt! and I just whitewashed the nursery.

JOSEPH: We will find him another.

MARY: All my life I wanted to make something of myself and I did, him. Say yes to him, Joseph.

JOSEPH: Yes.
(*He touches the babe's nose with a finger, looks up.*)
Oh God, who does not answer because he is all things and even our question is his answer, thank you.

MARY: Joseph, you're not—very logical—

(The song rises as they continue to walk in place, the light
loses them too, till only the star remains, the song dying away
to a whisper.)

CAST: The hopes and fears of all the
Hopes and fears of
Hopes and fears and
Hopes and
Hopes and
Hopes and
Hopes—

Blackout, silence.

MAN IN GREY

3 KINGS

3 LOUTS

COURIER

ANGEL

JOSEPH

TREE

HEROD

MARY

CHARACTERS

CHILDREN

GIRL

SHEEP   COW

DONKEY

2 WOMEN

3 KINGS
COW
SHEEP
TREE
2 WOMEN
MAN IN GREY
JOSEPH
MARY
GIRL
ANGEL
DONKEY

Other subsequent characters
are played by the above, as follows:

1st CHILD—COW
2nd CHILD, ACT I—DONKEY
COURIER—MAN IN GREY
3 LOUTS—3 KINGS
HEROD—MAN IN GREY
2nd CHILD, ACT II—SHEEP
2 SOLDIERS—2 KINGS

The animals must be played by children, not adults. Except
for the Man In Grey, the doublings are not to be recognizable;
in amateur production, with unpaid actors, they will not be
necessary. The Man In Grey however must play the Courier
and Herod, recognizably.

SET

The minimal set for the play consists of three platforms. Two, down right and down left, are box-size, and serve as seats and elevations for standing; they may be moved by the Cast for variety. The third, up center, is table-size, and may be used openly as a prop-table from which the actors pick up props as needed; if the production occurs in a church, the altar may serve this purpose, the rector willing. It should be large enough for actors to hide behind—the Angel and Cow when in Joseph's house, for instance, or Mary when giving birth in the stable.

These platforms may of course be elaborated by steps and other levels. In the play's professional premiere, the set included a high cross-walk at rear with ramps on either side, in amber raw wood, with a solid backing of newly-cut pines; the Cast moved in a few pieces of raw-wood furniture for Joseph's house, a throne and canopy for Herod, bales of hay for the stable, and burlap screens for an occasional backing—the screen which hid part of the stable was opened for a creche tableau.

The Cast may, at the director's discretion, sit throughout on benches at rear out of the lights; if so, the costume-changes in doublings—the Kings from the opening parade into the later Louts, the animals into the children—should be made offstage.

PROPS

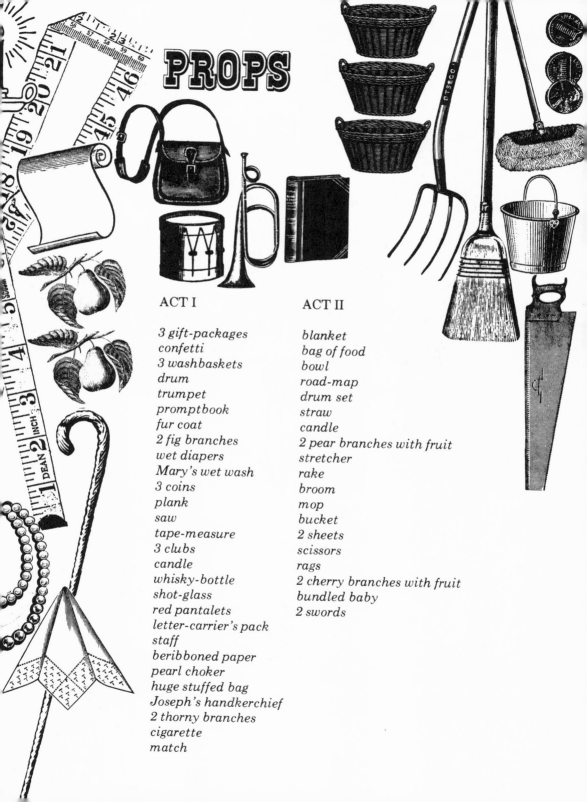

ACT I

3 gift-packages
confetti
3 washbaskets
drum
trumpet
promptbook
fur coat
2 fig branches
wet diapers
Mary's wet wash
3 coins
plank
saw
tape-measure
3 clubs
candle
whisky-bottle
shot-glass
red pantalets
letter-carrier's pack
staff
beribboned paper
pearl choker
huge stuffed bag
Joseph's handkerchief
2 thorny branches
cigarette
match

ACT II

blanket
bag of food
bowl
road-map
drum set
straw
candle
2 pear branches with fruit
stretcher
rake
broom
mop
bucket
2 sheets
scissors
rags
2 cherry branches with fruit
bundled baby
2 swords

WILLIAM GIBSON

author of *The Miracle Worker, Two for the Seesaw* and several
other plays, *A Mass for the Dead, A Season in Heaven* and
other books. He lives in Stockbridge, Massachusetts where he
has recently directed his own new play *The Body and the
Wheel*.

ELLEN KEUSCH

from Michigan by way of St. Mary's College, Notre Dame, In-
diana, is a widely-experienced professional designer whose ca-
reer includes a long stay as Art Director for a major interior
design magazine. Now she lives by the ocean.